MYSTERIOUS TALES *of* WESTERN NORTH CAROLINA

Sherman Carmichael

ILLUSTRATIONS BY LUCY ELLIOTT

THE
History
PRESS

Published by The History Press
Charleston, SC
www.historypress.com

Copyright © 2020 by Sherman Carmichael
All rights reserved

First published 2020

Manufactured in the United States

ISBN 9781467146470

Library of Congress Control Number: 2020938620

This book is dedicated to Beverly Carmichael, who spent many hours correcting my mistakes; Ric Carmichael; Tamara Carmichael; Blake Mahaffey; Sean Mahaffey; my attorney, Greg Askins; Cindy James; Lynette Goodwin; Troy Collins; and Cathy Sewell.

CONTENTS

CONTENTS

CONTENTS

HOW IT ALL BEGAN

It all began forty-eight years ago at the time of this writing (January 2020) with a copy of *Fate Magazine* and six boys with inquiring minds. There was my younger brother, Steve Carmichael; Mike Birchmore; Jason Birchmore; Earl Pope; Terry Owens; and me. Steve, Earl and Jason have long since gone home to meet their maker. As for Terry, I lost contact with him many years ago. Mike and I still stay in contact.

We set out looking for anything with a strange story tied to it. With two cars between us and very little money, we didn't do a whole lot of traveling back then and not very far either. I always had a 126 or a 110 camera with me. I never got a picture of anything, and to this day I still haven't, not even with all the sophisticated cameras that I've used over the years. Years later, we had our first encounter with the strange and unknown. I can't remember who was with me or the year, but we were at Old Gunn Church, where we heard the faint sound of a church choir singing their favorite hymn. The story of Old Gunn Church can be found in my third book, *Eerie South Carolina* (The History Press, 2013).

In 2010, Skip Lyle productions and Jim Holcomb got me to research South Carolina legends for a proposed TV series. After filming the first episode, Skip Lyle closed the project. With a file cabinet full of research, I had to decide what to do with it. I could chuck it away or write a book. So, I wrote a book. I'm still writing and plan to continue.

I imagine I've annoyed countless librarians, newspaper reporters, paranormal investigators, museum staff, property owners, ghost tour guides, historical societies and others in my quest for stories about the strange and unknown. And it all started with six young boys and an interest in the unknown.

JUST A THOUGHT

Let us explore the mysterious side of the North Carolina mountains. Let's step away from some of the most beautiful mountains in the United States and explore their little-known side, their darker side, their supernatural side. It's not surprising that the 480-million-year-old mountains would inspire legends and folk tales of every kind: strange lights in the sky… ghostly figures making an unexpected appearance from time to time…big hairy beasts that roam the mountains. And could the prince of darkness have made an occasional visit in the past? The mountains of North Carolina are a treasure-trove of mysterious legends.

When asked about ghosts or other unexplained things like Bigfoot, UFOs or strange lights, scientists and researchers drift off into self-made worlds of speculation, outrageous and unsubstantiated theories and impossible conclusions. There's nothing to prove that ghosts, Bigfoot or UFOs *don't* exist, but then there's nothing to prove that they *do* exist. As shown by history, every myth or legend reflects a real event, no matter how small.

Let's look at another possibility: that what we are seeing is not a ghost at all. Let's investigate this theory for a minute. What if what we're seeing is a glimpse of the past? For just a brief moment, we are standing at exactly the right place at the right time to see a glimpse of a past event. But then scientists say that the past doesn't exist in the present. Could they be wrong?

Since the 1940s, secret government agencies and civilian groups have been experimenting with time travel. One experiment was called the Montauk Project. Suppose the people involved found a way to bend time or create a portal or vortex through which a person could move through time and return to where he started from.

Why does a ghost haunt the same place—say, room 319 on the third floor of a hotel? Is there some attachment to that room? Is the ghost's spirit trapped there to perform the same task for eternity? Could that person have left an imprint in time? Do historical scenes that appear to certain people coexist with us in our time and *that's* what we think of as ghosts? If the ghost is the spirit of a dead person, then why are they still dressed in the clothes that they died in?

What about ghost ships, ghost planes, ghost cars and other ghost objects? They don't have spirits. Could two or more different groups of people be living in the same home in a different period? With all the theories and unsubstantiated facts, there is something to ghosts, whether or not it's the spirit of a dead person.

Do the spirits of the dearly departed endlessly relive former lives or events of the past? Why do these shadowy figures keep appearing without apparent reason from the dim corridors of the past? Maybe these wandering souls are nothing more than a bit of the history these people left behind. Ghosts or spirits—or whatever handle you put on them—have been around as far back as recorded history.

The power of a myth or legend is not in it being right or wrong but rather being believed. When doing research into the unknown, the trail leads us in many directions but ultimately into a world of the unknown where anything can happen.

When I was seventeen, I started dabbling in things that are best left alone, like ghosts, UFOs and monsters. I visited a lot of supposedly haunted places. I have continued to do so today. I have seen a lot of vandalism at historical places, including graveyards. I visited a historic church, and then several months later it was burned. Treat every place with respect. Don't vandalize.

I'm not trying to prove or disprove anything here. I'm just sharing the stories as I have found them. Belief or disbelief is up to you, dear readers. So sit back and enjoy this book and then take a trip and visit some of the places you have just read about. There's no telling who or what you will meet. Remember that some of these places are on private property, so please don't trespass.

DID THE DEVIL VISIT NORTH CAROLINA?

D id the devil drop in on North Carolina for a visit every now and then, or did he decide to hang around for a while? Did the early settlers name these places after the devil, or did the name come later—and for what reason? Why are so many locations linked to the devil? Was the naming of these places after the devil just coincidence, or was there a purpose behind the names?

Job 1: 6–7 (KJV) reads, "Now there was a day when the sons of God come to present themselves before the Lord and Satan also came among them, and the Lord said to Satan, 'From where do you come?' So Satan answered the Lord and said, 'From going to and fro on the earth and walking back and forth on it.'"

Town of Seven Devils

It's unknown which of the references to the devil was the reason for the name—or maybe it was all of them. One of the legends is that there was an old man who lived in the mountains who had seven sons, all as mean as the devil.

Locals commented about the harsh, cold winters, saying that the mountain was as cold as the devil or as windy as the devil. There were seven rocky peaks surrounding Valley Creek. On March 19, 1775, the government

opened up the Grandfather Mountain land for homesteading. The first known settler was Isaac McClurd from Scotland. He received two thousand acres at the head of the Watauga River.

In 1964, seven men on horseback—the four Reynolds brothers, Herb, Buck, Frank and Dan; Ray Smith; George Hampton; and Gardner Gidley— saw the mountain as something that should be shared by everyone. They braved an old wagon trail in one day to observe the seven peaks.

In 1965, the L.A. Reynolds Industrial District from Winston-Salem formed a resort. They wanted a catchy name that would bring attention to the mountain. They noticed the repeated mention of the number seven. The name Seven Devils seemed to suggest a resort where people could experience the temptations of seven devils.

The resort flourished until it was sold in 1972. A year later, the resort started having financial problems. In 1976, the resort went into bankruptcy. The resort club, acting as the property owners association, kept it running. A Greensboro business, Mountain Realty, bought the resort and worked with the residents to get the resort incorporated into the town of Seven Devils on June 30, 1979.

In 1980, the Mountain Group, headed by Robert Kent and Robert West, bought the resort from Chester Brown of Mountain Realty. Land was distributed to many individuals, completing the transition from resort to resort town.

The town of Seven Devils reached 5,200 feet and is in both Avery and Watauga Counties, surrounded by the great peaks of the Southern Appalachians and the Blue Ridge Mountains. Seven Devils is located across the valley from and within minutes of Grandfather Mountain. Seven Devils has some of the best views of Grandfather Mountain available anywhere in the region.

The Devil's Courthouse

The Devil's Courthouse overlook and trail is located on the Blue Ridge Parkway in the Blue Ridge Mountains in Transylvania County in Western North Carolina. The Devil's Courthouse is located at a height of 5,720 feet. It is located in the Nantahala National Forest ten miles northwest of Brevard, North Carolina. It is located at mile marker 422.4 on the Blue Ridge Parkway.

There is a moderate to strenuous half-mile climbing trail to reach the Devil's Courthouse. From the top, you can see North Carolina, South Carolina, Georgia and Tennessee.

Early settlers in the Smokies named the barren rock face the Devil's Courthouse. It may have received its name because of the sinister aspect of the rock formation. The legend goes that the devil held court in the cave beneath the rock. In Cherokee lore, the slant-eyed giant Judaculla dwells in the cave.

The Devil's Courthouse area is home to some rare and delicate high-altitude plants. Some of these Alpine species may be remnants from the glacial period. If you walk the trail, please stay on the trail and protect these rare plants, such as the Rock Gnome and the Spreading Avens.

The Devil's Stairs

In 1914, the Norfolk and Western Railroad extended the railroad from Abingdon, Virginia, into Ashe County, North Carolina. Construction for the railroad required a section of rock at the bend in the river to be dynamited. The demolition left a rock formation of four nearly perfect stairs, each nearly twelve feet high, ascending up the side of the mountain.

A railroad construction worker was killed in the blast. Parts of the worker were found in the surrounding woods for the next few days. Some believe that Satan had a hand in what happened, and the name the Devil's Stairs

was born. The Devil's Stairs acquired a macabre and somewhat mysterious character after the death of the worker.

The area is located on NC 194 north of West Jefferson in Ashe County, near the junction of Stanley Road. A bridge crosses Buffalo Creek. To the left of the bridge is the Devil's Stairs. It is located in Warrensville, North Carolina.

It seems that the haunting goes back farther than the date of the accident. One source says that before the area was settled, the Indians knew that the area was haunted. Details for this part of the story seem to be lost to time.

There are a number of ghostly legends that surround the Devil's Stairs. Sometime around the early 1900s, a man named Wilcox was headed home on his horse when he neared the stairs. Someone or something landed on the horse behind him. Two hairy arms wrapped around the man. The terrified horse began to run. About a half a mile down the road, they reached Oak Grove Church, where the thing vanished as quickly as it appeared. Mr. W.T. Dollar had the same experience. Something landed behind him on his horse. His horse ran down the road until it reached the church, and then the thing vanished.

There's the story of the phantom hitchhiker. A preacher was driving home after church services on a cold, rainy night when he approached the Devil's Stairs. He saw a person hitchhiking. The hitchhiker was wearing a long dark raincoat that covered most of his head and face. The preacher pulled over and offered the hitchhiker a ride. The figure never said a word as it got into the back seat. The preacher could not see the hitchhiker's face in the rearview mirror, so the preacher turned around and looked at the hitchhiker. Its eyes were as red as fire. When the preacher reached the destination, he stopped the car to let the rider out, but the rider was already gone.

Some of the locals say that the ghost of a girl in a prom dress has been seen in the area. According to some of the stories, when someone picks her up she will get into the car and then vanish when the driver pulls over to let her out. Many people have reported picking up hitchhikers only to have them vanish while passing the Devil's Stairs.

In the 1930s, a man lost his life when his car left the road near the Devil's Stairs. People have also reported hearing a voice singing old hymns as they walked along the railroad. Another story of tragedy in the area involves a mentally ill woman standing on a rock near the bridge and throwing her unwanted baby into the creek. A few days later, a fisherman reported hearing the cries of a baby along the bank.

The Devil's Whip

The Devil's Whip is the nickname for North Carolina State Road 80. It climbs 2,500 feet and crosses the Blue Ridge Parkway east of Mount Mitchell. The scenery along the Devil's Whip is beautiful and unimpeded by commercialism. There is nothing on this road. The amenities are in Marion at the entrance or in Burnsville, miles beyond the Blue Ridge Parkway.

The Devil's Whip is twelve miles long with 160 curves. When you hit the Learning Curve northbound (aka school bus turnaround), you've reached the point of no return.

BROWN MOUNTAIN LIGHTS

The Brown Mountain Lights are North Carolina's most famous lights. Brown Mountain is located at the foothills of the Blue Ridge Mountains in the northern part of Burke County in the Western North Carolina's Pisgah National Forest. You can find viewing areas at Linville Gorge on Linville Mountain, Wiseman's View, Lost Cove Overlook and Brown Mountain Overlook.

The Brown Mountain Lights are one of the most persistent mysteries in North Carolina. A United States Forestry Service sign marks the best area for viewing the Brown Mountain Lights. The lights have been seen from as far as fifteen miles away.

The lights gradually float to the top of the mountain, hover, pulsate brilliantly, change colors to reddish or blue and blink on and off before disappearing. The number of lights varies from one to hundreds. The lights may last for several minutes. They first appear as about twice the size of a star as they come up over the mountain. Sometimes they come up so thick and fast you can't count them.

The lights have been investigated by the United States Geological Survey, numerous scientists and historians since German engineer Gerald William de Brahm recorded them in 1771. A 1922 study by Georgia Tech made the most frequently made conclusion: the lights defy simple explanation.

In 1913, a United States Geological Survey studied the area and determined that witnesses had mistaken train lights for something more mysterious. Three years later, in 1916, a great flood swept through the

Catawba Valley and knocked out the railroad bridge. It was weeks before the railroad could be rebuilt. The lights continued to appear as usual.

In the 1950s, Scotty Wiseman wrote "Legend of the Brown Mountain Lights." This song was originally recorded by country duet Lula Bell and Scotty. In later years, Tommy Faile recorded the song.

The Brown Mountain Lights have been recorded since the earliest times. According to a legend handed down by the Cherokee Indians in the year 1200, a great battle was fought between the Cherokee and Catawba Indians. The Cherokees believe that the lights are the ghosts of the Indian maidens searching for their husbands or sweethearts who were lost in the great battle. Another version of this legend is that the Cherokee and Catawba Indians believe the lights are the spirits of the slain warriors.

Another legend begins on a night in 1850, when the wife of one of the locals mysteriously disappeared without a trace. The husband was the prime suspect, but with no evidence and no body, he could not be charged. One evening, a search party was out looking for her, but the forest wasn't revealing any clues. All of a sudden, strange lights appeared in the sky. Many of the local residents believe that the strange lights were the ghost of the man's wife coming back to haunt him. Shortly after the lights appeared, the man disappeared. After that, the lights disappeared for a while as well. A few years later, the skeleton of a woman was found by hunters. After the skeleton was found, the mysterious lights reappeared.

Another legend is that the lights are a troop of candle-bearing ghosts destined to march forever back and forth across Brown Mountain.

Another legend is one of a girl who lived on Brown Mountain with her father. Every night, her sweetheart would come see her. On the evening they were to leave to be married, she took a pine torch and went to meet him, but he never showed up. From that day on, she took her flaming torch and wandered the mountain looking for him. After her death, the light could still be seen on stormy nights.

Another version of the Brown Mountain Lights involves a wicked man named Jim, who was married to Belinda, who was soon in a family way. Jim was also courting a girl named Susie. Some neighbors noticed that they hadn't seen Belinda in a while and inquired as to her whereabouts. They were told that she was visiting some kinfolk. The neighbors' suspicions were aroused when they noticed bloodstains on the floor of Jim's cabin. The neighbors grew even more alarmed when they saw an indigent stranger drive away with Jim's horse and buggy. Shortly after that, Jim disappeared. Soon after that, the lights appeared. Later, under a pile of rocks in a ravine, the skeletons of a woman and a baby were found. Some believe that the lights were guiding searchers to the remains of Belinda and her baby. This incident occurred in the nineteenth century.

Theories

The lights have also been described as a manifestation of flying saucers. But another explanation is "Andes Lights," flashes of lightning discharging from clouds on the peaks of the Andes Mountains. The Brown Mountain Lights don't resemble lightning, though.

Other explanations are radium rays, foxfire, St. Elmo's fire, a chemical reaction between hydrogen sulfide and lead oxide, swamp gas (brief fires usually caused by methane gas discharge) and light reflections from nearby towns caused by warm and cold air mixing in the valley,

Earthquake lights, or earthlights, are a discharge of luminous balls of light from fault lines. A large fault line called Grandfather Mountain Fault runs directly under Brown Mountain. Earthquake lights are charged balls of plasma that shoot up from fault lines and are suspended in the air. This increases prior to an earthquake.

Some people believe that the lights are reflections from mountain moonshine stills.

One of the more famous theories of the Brown Mountain Lights comes from the tale of how a plantation owner went hunting and did not return. His trusted slave took a lantern and went in search of the plantation owner. Neither ever returned. The light is the slave still searching.

One report (and this is highly unlikely) says that during October 2011 hundreds of people saw the lights, videotaped and took pictures of them. More than twenty-seven people vacationing in a nearby camping area went missing that night, including three policemen. Of course, the alien theorists believe the government is involved in covering this up. Some UFO theorists believe that UFOs are responsible for the Brown Mountain Lights and that aliens have abducted six people out looking for the lights.

The lights are commonly seen on clear, dry nights in the fall. Moonless nights can aid visibility. The Brown Mountain Lights are a relatively rare occurrence now. No explanation given by any investigator so far has been deemed satisfactory. The Brown Mountain Lights formed one of *USA Today*'s Top 10 haunted spots in North Carolina.

Here is an interview I did with Johnny Stephens, unedited:

It's been many years since I saw the Brown Mountain Lights of North Carolina, but I still remember the experience vividly. It was 1974 and I was thirteen. For several summers, my aunt worked on her PhD at Appalachian State, and she rented a cabin near Boone. In June 1974, my family visited her for a week, and one night she took us to see the mysterious Brown Mountain Lights. It was a clear night, although there were no stars out. We drove to an overlook, where across the valley you could see Brown Mountain outlined against the night sky. As we stood against the railing, we did not have to wait long. After a few moments, the lights appeared. I remember there were several balls of light—perhaps six or seven—and they seemed to move in a slightly haphazard way across the face of the mountain. I had read that the best time to see them was in the fall, but on that June night they were perfectly clear. They didn't flicker or change size—they simply moved about the mountain in their own pattern. After a while, they began to grow dimmer, and we piled into my aunt's car and drove away. I do remember that I was reluctant to leave because it was so exciting for me to see one of the ghost stories I had read "come to life." Even as a boy, I knew I had encountered a true mystery. Over the years, I've thought many times about going back there, but I never have. Yet to this day, whenever the subject of ghost stories comes up and someone asks, "Have you ever seen a ghost?" I proudly answer, "Yes, I've seen the Brown Mountain Lights."

CAROLEEN BROAD RIVER BRIDGE

Like most haunted bridge stories, there's not a lot of information on the Caroleen Broad River Bridge. It is located in Rutherford County on US 221 alternate in Caroleen, North Carolina. The original bridge was replaced in the mid-1960s.

Some sources say that the bridge has been the site of a number of deaths and suicides over the years. Locals say that two elderly ladies driving home were killed when their car went off Caroleen Broad River Bridge. No date was given for the time of the accident, but the story goes something like this. On the night of the anniversary of their death, you can see the two elderly ladies walking toward home, which was about a half mile from the bridge.

Another story says that if you are driving by the bridge on rainy nights, you may see the two elderly ladies walking. If you give them a ride, they'll disappear from the back seat.

Another story associated with the Caroleen Broad River Bridge dates back to the 1950s. A woman described as beautiful with dark skin and red hair—many considered her the most beautiful woman they had ever seen—had previously been seen in the custody of the Forest City Police Department. She was later found strangled under the bridge.

There were several investigations into the circumstances of her death. The investigations supposedly ran into a dead end, and no arrest was ever made. There was no reason given as to why she was in custody in the first place, why she was no longer in custody or why she ended up dead under the bridge. There were rumors about who she was and why she had been locked up.

Shortly after the body was discovered, people began seeing her ghost on the bridge. Many people see her at night, and when they stop to offer her help, she vanishes.

HELEN'S BRIDGE

Helen's Bridge was built in 1909 to provide access to the Zealandia estate on the crest of the Beaucatcher Mountain in Asheville, North Carolina. It was originally built as a carriage way to and from the Zealandia mansion. The arch bridge was special from day one. The bridge was graced with beauty in its design and use of quarried stone. It is located over College Street between Windswept Drive and Beaucatchers Road.

In 1976, the existence of Helen's Bridge was threatened when the North Carolina Department of Transportation decided to make a cut through Beaucatcher Mountain for Interstate 240. The bridge was not in the path of the interstate, but it was feared that the shock waves from the construction blasting could damage or destroy the bridge.

Robert S. Griffin, principal architect with R.S. Griffin Architects P.A., lobbied for NCDOT to shore up the bridge during construction of the interstate. The department agreed to this and shored up the bridge with support scaffolding for extra support. The scaffolding remained in place for the next twenty-three years until the fall of 1999.

In 1999, there was talk by some individuals about tearing down the bridge, but they had opposition. There was strong support from the preservation community to repair and reopen the bridge to pedestrian traffic.

The preservation community won, but minor repairs were needed. Load tests needed to be done. Fearing that the bridge might collapse when the scaffolding was removed, they decided to lower the scaffolding two inches for the tests. If the bridge fell, it would only fall two inches. The bridge did

not fall, the load test was done and the bridge passed. The minor repairs were done, and the scaffolding was removed. Helen's Bridge was opened to pedestrian traffic.

Robert Griffin helped to form the Zealandia Committee, which raised $40,000 to help pay for the repairs and load tests. The City of Asheville donated $10,000, and the Asheville Public Works Department donated $3,685.

With all the beauty and history of Helen's Bridge, maybe there's another reason some people want to visit the bridge. Whatever the reason, enjoy the beauty.

There are several strange stories about deaths and ghosts associated with Helen's Bridge. Helen was a woman who lived near the bridge with her daughter. Helen worked on the estate and often brought her daughter to work with her. One day, she was called away from the room she was working in, leaving her daughter to play alone. When Helen returned, the room was on fire. Helen tried to rescue her daughter but was too late. Her daughter died in the fire. Helen, heartbroken by the death of her daughter, eventually hanged herself from the bridge. She returns to the bridge every full moon, trying to find her daughter. Some say if you go to the bridge and yell her name three times, Helen will appear. Sometimes you will have problems with your car when you get near the bridge.

Another version of the Helen story is that she appears to motorists when passing under the bridge. She is also said to wander around the bridge wearing a long flowing gown, asking people who are passing by if they've seen her daughter. Another story says that Helen was the mistress of one of the owners of the estate. After she found herself in a family way, she hanged herself.

One source says that researchers have found nothing to document the existence of an actual Helen.

THE MYSTERIOUS JUDACULLA ROCK

In the late 1800s, ethnologist James Mooney documented the Cherokee Indian legend of Tsul 'Kalu, the slant-eyed giant. As time passed, the name evolved into Judaculla. According to Cherokee legend, the markings on the rock were created by the Judaculla, the slant-eyed giant. This figure was more than seven feet tall, with seven fingers on each hand and seven toes on each foot. He was also very ugly and had a hairy body with clawlike fingernails and toenails. At one time, Judaculla took a human as his wife. The legend goes that Judaculla could also control the weather.

Within the Nantahala National Forest in Jackson County, North Carolina, in a pasture of 0.85 acres near the banks of Caney Fork, the mysterious Judaculla rock is seen jutting out of the earth. It is an outcropping of soapstone. The rock is covered with hundreds of ancient petroglyphs dating back to between two thousand and three thousand years ago. It predates the Cherokee Indians in this area. The petroglyphs have been studied by archaeologists and other researchers from across the world. No one has been able to decipher them or figure out who made them. Some archaeologists think that they were carved over the course of several centuries beginning five thousand years ago.

The entire mountain on which the rock is located is filled with a variety of metals and minerals that create detectable electromagnetic anomalies around the rock. A large vein of copper runs directly under the site. Early European settlers viewed the rock and the old field with superstition. Some insisted that the area was home to the Indian Satan.

There are 1,548 individual carvings that have been identified on the rock. The rock measures 240 square feet. The Judaculla rock contains more petroglyphs than any other known rock east of the Mississippi River. Some archaeologists have theorized that the Judaculla rock is a remnant of a prehistoric tribe who lived at the end of the ice age.

Due to the weather and some inconsiderate visitors, the rock is eroding. Judaculla rock is owned by Jackson County and can be visited during the day. In 2013, the Judaculla rock was added to the National Register of Historic Places.

Does the rock contain a secret coded message to mankind—if it does, what could it be?

CHIMNEY ROCK APPARITIONS

Chimney Rock is Rutherford's most widely known place. It is located in Hickory Nut Gorge, which includes several oddities itself. The mountain yields a deep and narrow entry into the Blue Ridge Country. Through the crevasse flows the Rocky Broad River and the US Routes 65–74. This is North Carolina's most spectacular gate to the western mountains. High above the gorge is the Chimney itself, standing 300 feet tall. Chimney Rock Mountain reaches 2,500 feet tall.

At the Bat Cave, the highway splits. US 74 continues across Hickory Nut Gorge to Asheville, while US 64 goes through Reedy Patch Gap to Hendersonville. The history of the gap as a thoroughfare goes back into Cherokee mythology. It's the story of the medicine man's trip through the gap to get the sacred tobacco.

One source says Hickory Nut Gorge was a battlefield between an Indian medicine man and the Little People. The Little People were guarding the pass and would not let the Native Americans through. The medicine man changed himself into a mole and burrowed under the gorge. He then changed himself into a whirlwind and moved through the gorge, tearing down cliffs and boulders, crushing the Little People. The medicine man got the tobacco and returned to the Cherokees. The boulders can still be seen today.

Oddities in the area include the Bat Cave and the Bottomless Pools. The cave is home to many bats generally as well as two rare species of bats. The pools are unusually large potholes credited to erosion at Pool Creek. Swift

water has found soft spots in the granite, mostly along faults or joints in the rock. Water was deflected from its forward path to form whirlpools. Stones caught in the whirlpools cut deep circular walls.

According to witnesses, strange apparitions have twice appeared on the mountain. The first people recorded to have witnessed the apparitions came on July 31, 1806, when Patsy Reeves and her children witnessed the strange, unearthly visitors. They saw a crowd of humanoid beings in varying sizes ranging in sizes from infants to adults clad in brilliant white raiment. The beings rose up and stopped on top of Chimney Rock. Then three members of the group rose above the others and seemed to lead the unearthly congregation of shining beings up through the air, disappearing into the heavens. There were six people in the group that witnessed this spectacular event.

Five years later, in 1811, two troops of ghostly cavalry, men on winged horses, seemed to appear out of nowhere, appearing in the same place, and engaged in a battle in the sky. Five people witnessed this ghostly battle and reported that they could hear the clashing of the swords and the moans of the wounded. The battle was fought over Chimney Rock and lasted for about ten minutes. The defeated army retreated, and the winning army disappeared into the darkness. Today, many people blame a space-time break where they witnessed a battle of the not-too-distant Revolutionary War, albeit with winged horses.

An Indian medicine man, ghostly cavalrymen on winged horses, angels ascending into the heavens, space-time breaks and who knows what other mysteries all circle Chimney Rock.

GRANDFATHER MOUNTAIN'S PHANTOM HIKER

Grandfather Mountain, North Carolina, got its name from the unique and distinct formation on its top. The formation resembles the head of a bearded old man lying down asleep. It is 5,946 feet in elevation and has a fantastic view of the Blue Ridge Mountains. According to some guidebooks, there are sixteen distinct ecosystems on Grandfather Mountain. The unique and gorgeous natural environment around the mountain makes it a big drawing card for visitors. Grandfather Mountain had long been operated as a private tourist attraction until 2011, when the State of North Carolina bought it. It is now a publicly owned nature preserve.

Grandfather Mountain has a special place in Cherokee mythology. It is called Tanawha and was once considered the resting place of the eagle spirit. Another legend from Grandfather Mountain is that it holds an entrance to the underworld, marked by a spring and guarded by the Little People.

The park has eleven trails that cover miles of mountainous terrain. The more difficult backcountry trails take you through some unique ecosystems and are home to many rare and endangered plant species.

On one of the trails, something far rarer has been seen: the Phantom Hiker. There is some disagreement on which trail is the Phantom Hiker's. The description given by most who have had the pleasure of encountering the Phantom Hiker is an older bearded man with a rough, grizzly appearance. The Phantom Hiker is dressed in old-fashioned work clothes from possibly the middle of the twentieth century. He is always wearing an old army backpack and carrying a long walking stick. Some believe that the Phantom

Hiker was just an old man who died in the area and refused to leave, even after death. Some believe that he might have been an explorer who fell from the mountain.

The Phantom Hiker appears mostly as the evening shadows start to creep in. He never says anything to anyone or acknowledges anyone's greetings. He appears on the trail walking, moves ahead of everyone else and then vanishes.

Why does this shadowy figure keep appearing from the dim corridors of the past? Is the Phantom Hiker suspended in time and destined to hike Grandfather Mountain forever?

SIREN OF THE FRENCH BROAD RIVER

The legend of the Siren of the French Broad River dates back to 1845. The Lorelei is a siren that appears in the river to hikers and travelers who venture close by. The weary camper who is trying to settle down for the night finds himself troubled by strange dreams. The night is long and almost sleepless as a beautiful, dark-haired, dark-eyed woman walks in and out of his mind.

He wakes before dawn and goes down to the river to refresh himself. He hears this soft, exquisite, enchanting voice blending with the sound of the river splashing against the river bank. The unsuspecting camper looks into the water and sees the faint though distinct form of a beautiful woman with dark hair flowing in the water. He cannot resist. He reaches into the river. The arms that grab him are not the arms of the beautiful woman. They are as slimy and cold as a serpent. The beautiful smiling face that was staring up at him is now a grinning skull.

This is an American Indian story. It first appeared in print in 1845 as "Tzelica, A Tradition of the French Broad," a poem by William Gilmore Simms.

DILLSBORO VAMPIRE

In the spring of 1788, Dr. Alfort, his wife and their fifteen-year-old son moved into the quiet, peaceful small mountain community of Dillsboro, North Carolina They purchased some land and built a large colonial-style home near the Tuckasegee River. Dr. Alfort set aside several rooms on the first floor for his office and apothecary.

Rumors started circulating around the small community that the Alfort family were descendants of royalty. Whether the rumors were true, the townsfolk were happy to have a doctor living in the community. He had many patients, and life was going well until two of his patients met unfortunate deaths. They had visited the doctor for gout. Both patients were well-liked members of the town. Many of the townspeople considered the deaths suspicious. Many were angry about them.

The minster managed to calm the accusers who were pointing fingers at Dr. Alfort. The minister explained that in the sight of God, no one is promised tomorrow.

Dillsboro returned to normal until fall arrived. One day in the fall, the minister's wife entered their children's room. She said she saw a dark figure hovering above the young daughter's bed. The mother screamed and rushed to the daughter, only to find her dead. Other members of the household rushed to the room. No one could say where the dark figure went. When Dr. Alfort examined their daughter, the only signs were two puncture marks on the girl's neck and small drops of blood on the pillow near her neck.

The peaceful little community of Dillsboro was turned upside down with rumors of vampires. Every night, search parties were sent out in search of the elusive night creature. People reported seeing a huge batlike creature flying around one night. They started believing that vampires were on the loose, leading many to close their doors and windows at night. Families were afraid to leave their children alone in their rooms, especially after nightfall.

One night, a young boy ran to his grandfather's house to tell him that something was in his home attacking his mother and father. The grandfather and a group of neighbors rushed up to the house. When they entered the house, they found the mother, father and two young'uns dead. The only visible signs of violence were puncture marks on the necks of the four people.

The people in the surrounding community were notified, and a thorough search immediately got underway. The search party found nothing. Several soldiers were called in to search the community, but they came up empty.

By February 1789, things had gotten back to normal. The residents of Dillsboro had finally convinced themselves that the vampire—or whatever committed the brutal murders—was dead or moved on. Then one evening, it all began again when a scream was heard coming from a neighbor's house. A group of men rushed to the house just in time to see a dark shadow come out of the house and make its way to Dr. Alfort's house. The two people in the house were found dead with puncture marks on their necks.

A group of men rushed over to Dr. Alfort's house, but the doctor refused to let them in. A group of men stood guard outside of the doctor's house while others went for the sheriff and reenforcements.

When the sheriff arrived, the group forced its way into the house, removed Dr. Alfort from the home and tied him to a tree. When they entered the house, they found a lot of strange things. There were bed chambers on the second floor with beds that appeared not to have been used. Downstairs three caskets were found. Mrs. Alfort, dressed in black, was inside one of the caskets. However, she was very much alive. The son was not found in the house at all. One source says that the caskets were found in the cellar.

Later that night, a verdict was reached, and the sheriff and village minister announced in front of the Alforts' home that the Alforts were vampires. They hanged the Alforts, placed their dead bodies back in the house and burned it to the ground. The fifteen-year-old boy was never seen again. That was the end of the gruesome murders.

Were the Alforts really vampires, or did innocent people die because of mass hysteria? Are there real vampires? There will always be a question behind this troubling mystery.

DEMON DOG

There is not much information to back up this story. No historical data or dates lend any credit to the tale of the Demon Dog. One source says that it's one of the most frightening apparitions in the catalogue of North Carolina hauntings. This strange case comes from the quiet mountain town of Valle Crucis. I could only find a single record of a single sighting.

Valle Crucis, which is Latin for "Valley of the Cross," got its name because of the two streams that meet in the middle of the valley to form a cross. Some say that the morning mist lingers longer in the valley than anywhere else in the mountains. The quietness sets Valle Crucis off from the rest of the world.

Valle Crucis is best known for the popular Mast General Store tourist attraction. There is also a beautiful rustic stone church and cemetery located on the edge of town on Highway 194. At night, from among the graves in the churchyard cemetery, something emerges that might combine earth and hell. A mysterious shadow wanders around the graveyard and then emerges onto the road.

The only incident I've found about this mysterious creature was one night when two men were driving past the church. The creature jumped out into the road ahead of them. The full moon was bathing the valley in an eerie glow. With the moon and the car headlights, visibility was good. The driver slammed on brakes, pulling the car to the side of the road. They described the animal as a giant dog covered with bristling black fur and showing its massive yellow teeth. The creature's eyes were glowing red, something like the very fires of hell—not at all like a dog's eyes reflecting light.

The unearthly beast started walking toward the car, and the driver roared off past the creature, leaving it in the dust. As the car sped away, the driver looked into the rearview mirror to see where the creature was. To his shock, the ghostly dog was keeping up with the car traveling sixty to seventy miles per hour. Then ghostly dog began gaining on the car. Just as the car crossed the bridge where the two streams meet to form a cross, the ghost dog stopped and vanished.

HOT SPRINGS

Hot Springs, North Carolina, has been a resort destination since the early 1800s. It became famous for its healing hot mineral springs. The town received its name from those springs. Hot Springs is just forty minutes north of Asheville, located at the junction of the Appalachian Trail and the French Broad River. The valley is surrounded by the Blue Ridge Mountains and the Pisgah National Forest. Hot Springs is North Carolina's only town where the Appalachian Trail runs directly down Main Street.

Hot Springs was voted the Best Small Mountain Town from Georgia to West Virginia by the readers of the *Blue Ridge Outdoors Magazine*.

American Indians were the first to discover the one-hundred-plus-degree mineral water springs. Traders from the colonies came next, and in 1778, the lame and sick were traveling to Hot Springs for the healing waters. On March 19, 1791, William Nelson bought the hot springs property for £200 in Virginia currency and turned it into a tourist destination.

In 1831, James Patton of Asheville bought the springs. By 1837, Patton had built a hotel with 350 rooms. The new hotel was called Patton's White House. The luxurious dining room could seat six hundred people.

James Rumbough bought hot springs in 1862. In 1882, the railroad reached the village. Due to the number of people arriving on the train, Rumbough decided to enlarge the hotel. In 1884, Patton's White House burned down. As a result, the springs and much of the town were sold to the Southern Improvement Company.

In 1886, the Mountain Park Hotel was constructed. Shortly after that, a higher-temperature springs was discovered. Hot Springs was now one of the most elegant resorts in its day. The area included a two-hundred-room hotel, a barn, a stable, a spring house and a bathhouse with sixteen marble pools. The Mountain Park Hotel established the first organized golf club in the Southeast.

Hot Springs is now a haven for people looking for relaxation and a healthful mountain retreat. The town has often been referred to as "Where Mayberry meets the Twilight Zone."

There are a few ghost stories that go along with Hot Springs. Many people have witnessed the ghost of a Cherokee Indian man near the springs. One report says that while a couple were enjoying the Jacuzzi in their room, the ghost of a woman grabbed the woman's arm, trying to pull her out of the tub. Minutes later, she was grabbed again. Others have reported being grabbed by the woman and have smelled cigarette smoke. No one ever reported seeing the woman that was grabbing them. The room is now formally called the Vance room, but for those who have experienced something unusual, know it simply as "Room 1." People reported seeing the figure of a Cherokee man walking in the woods near the river and the springs. Some while soaking in the hot tub reported a ghost joining them in the tub.

In 1884, Patton's White House burned. In 1920, the Mountain Park Inn burned. And in 1977, the Hot Springs Inn burned.

Today, hikers can explore the scenic Appalachian Trail, which runs 2,100 miles. Rafters can navigate the rapids on the French Broad River. Those coming to simply to relax can enjoy the area's scenery while taking a relaxing dip in a hot mineral bath.

DEAD DAN'S SHADOW

Shadows or shadowy figures have always been a primary part of ghost lore. You see shadows lurking around the corner. You see a glimpse of them from the corner of your eye, and you see them moving around. This story is about another kind of shadow.

Daniel Keith was wrongfully accused of the brutal death of an eight-year-old Rutherford County girl. The report said that the girl had been beaten to death with a rock. Keith was arrested and jailed on the flimsiest of evidence. The sheriff found a shirt on Keith's back porch with bloodstains on it. The shirt was in plain sight. Keith said that he had worn the shirt while cleaning rabbits.

Sheriff N.E. Walker said that Keith was sober at the time of the arrest. Keith kept repeating that he didn't know anything about the death of the little girl.

This was a time in North Carolina's history when corporal punishment was carried out in a public place for anyone who wished to see. Many men and women were convicted on very little evidence.

On November 8 or 9, 1880, Daniel Keith went to the courthouse in Rutherfordton, North Carolina. The good citizens of Rutherford County's lust for justice outweighed their sense of responsibility for a fair trial. A witness reported seeing Daniel Keith near the child's home on that day. Other witnesses reported that he had been drinking the day of the child's death. A sixteen-year-old boy swore that he heard a little girl scream and saw Keith running away from the area with blood on his hands. The shirt

the boy testified that Keith was wearing was not the shirt that the sheriff found at Keith's house. Daniel Keith took the witness stand to declare his innocence, but in less than an hour the jury returned with a guilty verdict.

Before the judge sentenced him, Keith was allowed to speak. "Those who said I killed anyone is a liar. Each one of you will be haunted for the rest of your lives. Then the devil will have his day with you."

Keith was sentenced to hang on December 11, 1880. It was a cold December day as the crowds gathered along the street to see another human die. While Keith stood on the gallows, he was allowed to speak his final words. "The soul of an innocent man doesn't rest." The hangman put the rope around his neck, and the sack was placed over his head. At one o'clock, Daniel Keith was hanged.

There was no shrieking ghost, no mysterious lights, no disembodied voices—just a shadow. The shadow of a hanging man has appeared on the south wall of the jail. The shadow remained on the jailhouse wall after he was taken down. Keith was held in the south part of the jail.

People who witnessed the hanging returned to Rutherfordton to see the shadow. Everyone who saw the shadow said it was the shadow of Daniel Keith. So many people were coming to see the shadow that the town decided to paint over it. That didn't work, so it tried to scrub it off the wall. The only thing that did was to scrub the paint off the wall. Nothing worked—the shadow remained. Again they tried painting it. This time they used several coats of paint, but with no success. The shadow remained so clear that it was visible at night.

The jail was eventually sold and turned into a private residence. The new owners, in another attempt to cover the shadow, planted ivy. The ivy eventually grew up and covered the wall, but the shadow remained. The shadow continued to haunt those who testified against Keith and the jury that convicted him.

In 1949, two things happened in Rutherfordton that ended the story of the shadow of the hanging man on the wall and put Daniel Keith to rest. The private residence was once again sold and turned into an office building. The ivy on the south wall was torn down, and several coats of paint were applied. The shadow did not return. The other thing that happened was that an eighty-five-year-old man passed away. He had been the sixteen-year-old boy who testified against Keith in 1880. He was the last of those cursed by Daniel Keith.

THE PHANTOM RIDER
OF THE CONFEDERACY

The ghostly apparition of a girl on horseback can still be seen around the Calvary Episcopal Church in Fletcher, North Carolina. The church is known for more than its welcoming and faithful congregation. It's also known for a ghost. While the church does not play host to the ghost, the surrounding area does.

The phantom rider is the ghost of a young woman that rides a palomino horse. She has flowing blond hair and is wearing a long white dress and a gray Confederate cape.

The story begins with two young sweethearts. The girl's parents did not approve of her having a relationship with this boy, so they had to meet in secret. They met at the old well at the church. It was in the 1860s, as the Civil War raged on. Her sweetheart was called to join the Confederate army. He would be serving under Confederate general Braxton Bragg and the Army of Tennessee.

The girl's parents would not allow the young couple to get married before her sweetheart was sent off to war. One day, the young woman received word that her soldier had died in battle. Devastated by the news of his death, she went to their old meeting place. Broken-hearted, she wished she could join him in death. Within two months, she had died.

In the spring of 1865, as the Civil War was winding down, Union general George H. Stoneman came through the mountains of North Carolina. The general was trying to put down any Confederate resistance left. The Union army was patrolling near Fletcher, North Carolina, when soldiers spotted

a young woman riding a horse. Believing that she might have valuable information about the Confederate soldiers, they set out after her. None of the Union army could catch up with her. She led the Union army into a small ravine a short distance from the church. The army rode straight into a Confederate ambush. Twenty-three Union soldiers were killed. The Confederates suffered only a few casualties. This was the first encounter with the phantom rider of the Confederacy.

Union general Stoneman was so enraged that he organized a search party. Each time they saw the phantom rider, they could never catch her. When they got close enough to shoot her, it seemed as if the bullets were just passing through her. She would then disappear from sight. She has been seen many times riding down the roads around the Calvary Episcopal Church. One of the witnesses was at the time the minister of the church.

If you're out on Old Fletcher Road at night and see the phantom rider of the Confederacy, beware following her. She may lead you into impending doom. She has been seen many times by reliable witnesses.

1907 ALTA PASS RAILROAD TUNNEL EXPLOSION

On a Saturday in May 1907, at about 4:00 p.m., an explosion in a tunnel at the foot of Lookout Mountain on the Stevenson extension of the South & Western Railway killed nine construction workers. The crew was blasting rock deep inside the tunnel. The crew prepared and set three explosives. Two went off. Some of the crew, thinking that all three had

exploded, returned to the tunnel to work. Just as the crew got started, the third explosive went off, hurling the thirteen-man crew into the air and nine to their deaths. The four other crew members died shortly after.

Foreman Jack Hyder and a crew of twenty men were blasting a tunnel for the South & Western Railway. The other seven workers hauling rock outside were stunned by the blast. When they recovered enough, they rushed inside the tunnel to help the injured. After entering the tunnel, they found the ground covered with lifeless bodies.

The powerful blast wrecked a bridge and sent a freight engine and eleven cars through the bridge and into the Chattanooga Creek. The bridge was crushed by several tons of rock.

The explosion also hurled rocks four hundred yards, killing two men in a pile driver. The pile driver was driving piles in the Chattanooga Creek for a new viaduct. Houses more than a quarter of a mile away were heavily damaged. Residences on the side of Lookout Mountain suffered roof and floor damage as rocks came crashing through the roofs.

The men on the crew working for the railway company were natives of the Alta Pass, North Carolina area.

1890 MELROSE TRAIN WRECK

A very destructive train wreck happened in June 1890 on the Western North Carolina Railroad near Melrose Station. The accident occurred on the south side of Saluda Mountain, where there is a steep down grade about six hundred feet. An extra engine is kept at this location to help trains up or down the mountain.

The railroad track was very wet when the coal train with twelve fully loaded cars started down the mountain. It soon became evident that the two engines were no match for the twelve loaded coal cars. Even with the brakes on both engines being held down, the train reached a speed of seventy-five miles per hour. The tracks spread, sending the two engines and twelve coal cars down the mountain, burying the engines beneath broken coal cars, coal, crossties and earth.

A train was dispatched from Asheville, North Carolina, with Superintendent McBee and several surgeons to the scene of the accident. When the train returned, it was carrying the bodies of the men who stood their post in an attempt to save the train. Three were killed and five injured in the wreck.

1948 ASHEVILLE HIGHLAND MENTAL HOSPITAL FIRE

Around midnight on March 10, 1948, a fire broke out in the diet kitchen of the women's building of the Highland Mental Hospital. The fire roared through the hospital building, taking the lives of nine female patients. Twenty of the female patients were led out of the building to safety. The fire quickly engulfed the four-story building.

Police Captain Harold Enloe was the first to arrive on the scene. Firemen, policemen, doctors, nurses and some of the local townspeople rushed to the rescue. Every available piece of firefighting equipment the city had was rushed to the scene. Off-duty firemen also rushed to the scene. Seven of the women were trapped on the upper floors and were unable to escape. Two were removed by firemen but shortly died.

Betty Uboenga and Frances Render first rescued and assisted the helpless patients. After they had aided them, they returned to assist the other patients but found that some had been trapped.

This was the third fire in the hospital in less than a year. Two broke out in April. One fire started from a mattress and the other from oil-soaked rags carefully placed under the stairway. Arson was suspected, but no one was ever charged.

Zelda Fitzgerald, wife of F. Scott Fitzgerald, died in the fire. She never completed her second novel.

In 1939, the founder of the Highland Hospital for Nervous Disease, Dr. Robert S. Carroll, entrusted the hospital to the Neuropsychiatric Department of Duke University. Duke owned the property until the 1980s.

Today, the complex functions as an office park and shopping plaza.

1955 CHEROKEE
FOOT BRIDGE COLLAPSE

On July 3, 1955, a foot bridge on the Cherokee Indian Reservation collapsed, sending an estimated one hundred people ten to fifteen feet down onto the jagged rocks and into the shallow stream of the Oconaluftee River. The 150-foot bridge fell shortly before noon on July 3. Many of the pedestrians who fell were also struck by falling bridge timber, cables and other victims, adding to their injuries. People who were on the riverbanks prevented anyone from drowning.

The bridge formed a walkway from US 441 to a group of souvenir shops located on the Cherokee Indian Reservation.

The injured were taken to the hospitals by ambulances and private automobiles. Five people were listed in critical condition. Many others were hospitalized, and forty-eight people received first aid at the scene. Two people died from the fall.

Chief Osley Bird Sunanooke of the Eastern Band of Cherokee said that tribal officials who were in charge of the bridge posted guards on the bridge to prevent the overcrowding on the bridge. But the eager visitors and tourists paid no attention to the guards' instructions.

A letter from the Department of the Interior Information Services Office of the Secretary dated July 6, 1955, noted that "the accident is reported to have been caused by children jumping on the Indian Bridge which caused it to buckle and throw about sixty sightseers into the bed of the Oconaluftee River." It was signed M.M. Tozier, Indian Bureau, room 4142.

1916 LAKE TOXAWAY DAM FAILURE

Western North Carolina gained national recognition in the late 1800s as a vacation center for the wealthy. The area was made more accessible when the railroad came in.

A group of Pittsburgh businessmen formed a company called the Toxaway Company in 1895 to acquire and develop land and mine any minerals found on the land. The company began to build summer resorts in the "Switzerland of America."

Lake Fairfield, an eighty-acre lake, was constructed and the Fairfield Inn was added in 1896. The next project was Lake Sapphire. When Lake Sapphire was completed in 1897, the Lake Sapphire Inn was built. In 1900, the two-hundred-room Franklin Hotel was constructed. The next project for the Toxaway Company was to dam the Toxaway River, creating the biggest man-made lake in the Appalachian Mountains. Work began on the dam on June 1, 1902, and was completed in the middle of July 1903. The dam was sixty feet long and five hundred feet wide, making Lake Toxaway three miles long, one mile wide and thirty feet deep, covering 550 acres. Construction continued on the Lake Toxaway area with the construction of the five-story Toxaway Inn. The inn had the most modern conveniences of the time, including central heat, private indoor plumbing and elevators.

In 1904, the Transylvania Railroad extended the rail line to the Lake Toxaway depot. Shortly after the railroad came in, the depot started receiving four trains a day. It also had a stage line where passengers could take a stagecoach and travel to other resort areas farther up the mountain.

In 1908, the Toxaway Hotel began to show signs of struggling. In 1912, the Toxaway Company's largest shareholder, Edward H. Jennings, bought the company and made needed improvements to the hotel. Jennings began selling land parcels around the lake for private homes.

A flood in 1916 would change Lake Toxaway forever. After suffering two hurricanes in July, Lake Toxaway was hit by another hurricane from the Gulf of Mexico. Lake Toxaway received more than twenty inches of rain in a twenty-four-hour period.

At 7:10 p.m. on August 13, there was a catastrophic failure of the dam. Lake Toxaway dam burst, sending more than 5.3 billion gallons of water downstream through the Toxaway River Valley into western South Carolina. Residents reported seeing a thirty-foot-tall wave of water that left debris and huge rocks nearly four miles downstream. Rocks as big as train cars were moved by the water.

Anderson, Walhalla, Pickens and Seneca Counties composed the territory threatened by the water. Portman Shoals, where the electric power for the city of Anderson came from, was preparing to combat the anticipated floodwaters. A few houses were destroyed, but the only casualty attributed to the dam failure was one blind mule.

The Lake Toxaway Hotel never reopened.

GHOSTS OF THE BILTMORE HOUSE

In 1862, George Washington Vanderbilt was born in Staten Island, New York. George was the grandson of famed industrialist and philanthropist Cornelius Vanderbilt. Cornelius started his career at the age of sixteen by ferrying people and goods across the waters of Staten Island and Manhattan. After years of hard work, Cornelius Vanderbilt built a vast system of shipping and railroads. When he died, he left his family about $100 million.

In 1888, at the age of twenty-five, George Vanderbilt and his mother traveled to the Blue Ridge Mountains of North Carolina. Vanderbilt found the perfect place for his country home. He bought 125,000 acres near Asheville.

The beauty of the Biltmore estate was due to the combined efforts of three men: George Vanderbilt; Richard Morris Hunt, architect (1828–1895); and Frederick Law Olmsted, the father of landscape architecture in America (1822–1903).

In 1889, construction began on the Biltmore house complex. This included the Biltmore home, gardens, farms and woodlands. The home was modeled after two other very impressive houses: one in Buckinghamshire, England, called the Waddesdon Manor and the other the Chateau de Blois in the Loire Valley in France.

A three-mile railroad track was built to connect the main railroad line to the location of the house in order to ship in material. Hundreds of laborers and craftsmen were hired to construct the Biltmore house.

The centerpiece was a four-story stone house with a 780-foot façade. It had a stair tower and steeply pitch roof. More than 11 million bricks were used in the construction. It had a spiral staircase that reached four floors and had 102 steps and an iron chandelier that contained seventy-two electric bulbs. It used some of Edison's first lightbulbs.

The second and third floors contained luxurious bedrooms and an area where guests played parlor games and had afternoon tea. The fourth floor contained the maid's bedrooms and the observatory. Downstairs was the domestic nerve center: the main kitchen, two specialty kitchens and the refrigeration system. It was fully electric and centrally heated. It had a fire alarm system, two elevators, indoor plumbing for all thirty-four bedrooms and a telephone. It had sixty-five fireplaces and more than four acres of floor space. There was a swimming pool, a gym and a bowling alley in the house.

In 1895, the Biltmore was open to friends and family on Christmas Eve. Vanderbilt's mother, Maria Louisa Kissam Vanderbilt, lived with him and helped him host when guests came to visit.

George Vanderbilt wanted the estate to be self-sustaining. He had herds of sheep, swine, poultry and cattle brought in. He had gardens and nurseries planted. He was an avid book collector and spent many hours in the library reading.

In 1898, Vanderbilt married Edith Stuyvesant Dresser in Parris. The couple honeymooned in Italy and then returned to Biltmore to live. On August 22, Cornelia Vanderbilt was born in the Louise XV room. In 1914, George Vanderbilt passed away at the age of fifty-one. He is buried in the Vanderbilt Family Mausoleum on Staten Island, New York. In 1924, Cornelia Vanderbilt married the Honorable John Francis Amherst Cecil, a British diplomat. They were married at the All Souls Church in Biltmore Village. In 1925, John and Cornelia Vanderbilt Cecil's first son, George Henry Vanderbilt Cecil, was born. In 1928, John and Cornelia's second son was born in the Louis XV room.

In 1930, the Biltmore was opened to the public. People could tour the house and gardens. Rare Franklinia and Persian Ironwood trees grow along with mountain laurel, rhododendron, azaleas and white pines. Plants bloom in the Biltmore gardens from March through November. The four-acre walled gardens features fifty thousand tulips, summer annuals and a host of chrysanthemums. The rose garden contains more than 250 varieties of roses. While visiting the Biltmore, see the Biltmore Winery, the Barn Door, A Christmas Past, Book Binders, the Gate House, A Garden's Place and a host of other interesting sites.

The Ghosts of the Biltmore

Workers keep reporting seeing a shadowy figure in the library, usually when a storm is coming. Could this be the ghost of George Vanderbilt? People passing through have reported hearing a woman's voice whispering "George." People have reported hearing the gentle sound of glasses being struck together, laughter when no one's around and music and water splashing coming from a now empty pool. Another ghost is the weeping lady in black. No one knows who she is or why she's crying. Some have reported hearing footsteps.

Some people have reported hearing George and Edith laughing and talking near the fireplace. Servants have noticed the presence of George Vanderbilt in his favorite sitting room on the second floor.

THE PHANTOM CHOIR

Roan Mountain sits on the border of North Carolina and Tennessee. Roan Mountain is not just one mountain—it's a five-mile-long ridgetop that reaches nearly two miles above sea level at Roan High Top. It offers some of the most beautiful views in the Southeast. Roan Mountain is covered with balsams and rhododendrons that fill the hills with spectacular patches of pink and white flowers when in bloom.

There is a mystery to Roan Mountain. Some say that the wind on Roan Mountain carries more than a fall chill or summer storm. There is a haunting music that can be heard along the mountain. The ghostly music was heard long before white men came to America. Some say it's a choir of ghosts left from the battlefield of past Indian wars. Others say that it's from the earliest days of European settlers. Some people who have come to Roan Mountain have reported hearing a song not of this world traveling on the devil wind. The wind is powerful on Roan Mountain and can carry sounds forever. In the early nineteenth century, the stories that began coming from the mountain told that as the wind whipped around, it carried something else with it. You could hear voices singing in the wind.

No one can agree on what king of singing it is. Some say the singing was the sound of an angelic choir, the voices of heavenly beauty. Others say it's the sound of angels rehearsing for the end of the world, while others say it's the angels gathering to practice their song for the Christian Judgment day. There are also the ones who say that when you're on Roan Mountain you can hear the sounds of heaven.

Others disagree. They say it's the unearthly wailing of demons and tormented souls crying out. There are others who will tell you that it's the echoes from hell. Could it be the voices of the Catawba Indians who fought and died on Roan Mountain calling out?

A young man hiked into the mountains one gloomy day and got caught in a raging thunderstorm. He began hearing unearthly howls and moans in the air. As he searched for shelter from the storm, the sound continued. Finally he found a cave. He found what he believed to be shelter inside the cave, but he was unnerved when the air filled with visions of tortured bodies swirling around him. Their screams of torment were all he could hear. The hiker was convinced that he had taken a look through the doors of hell.

No one can agree on what the sounds are or where they're coming from. All they can agree on is that the phenomenon is coming from Roan Mountain. The sounds are heard most after a thunderstorm.

Another legend about Roan Mountain is that the Catawba Indians challenged the other tribes in the area to a battle. The battle was so bloody that at the edge of the bald the rhododendrons when in bloom were bright red.

Many people have seen a circular rainbow in the sky above Roan Mountain. This is a natural phenomenon. Roan Mountain has the right conditions to make it one of the few places on the planet where that can happen.

THE BIGFOOT MYSTERY

Bigfoot or Sasquatch (or whatever name it is called) has been seen for many years in the mountains of North Carolina and nearly every other state in the United States. Researchers spend countless thousands of dollars on equipment to try to locate a Bigfoot or at least get proof of such a beast. Countless hours have been spent in the woods by investigators and ordinary people.

So far, no one has found any physical evidence, and no reliable photographs have been taken. There is no evidence to prove there's a Bigfoot, except eyewitness testimony of reliable people who believe they have seen the mystical creature.

Why is Bigfoot there and then suddenly gone? There is the theory that Bigfoot is a genetically engineered bear that has reproduced with ordinary bears, producing a much larger species. Of course, there are other theories, like that it's an interdimensional creature or an alien. Of course, the best theory is it's just an animal that's always been around and doesn't stay in one place very long.

Burke County Bigfoot

On June 26, 2013, a witness was driving home on Frank Whisnant Road in Burke County, North Carolina, from a fishing trip at Lake James. Lake

James is in the Pisgah National Forest. It was between 1:30 a.m. and 2:00 a.m. when he spotted something moving on the embankment behind the guardrail. He only saw the head and shoulders. Its facial features were almost humanlike. It had very broad shoulders. Its hair was four to six inches long and reddish brown. The skin was darker than its body hair. The sighting lasted about ten seconds as he drove by with his bright lights on. His aunt was in the car but wasn't sure if she saw anything.

It was a clear summer night, with the temperature being about sixty-three degrees. The moon was crescent.

APPALACHIAN STATE UNIVERSITY GHOST

Appalachian State University's East Hall dormitory appears to be just another residence hall, but there is another side, or so the students say.

The story began in the early 1960s in Boone, North Carolina, when the university was still Appalachian Teachers College. It all began on the lowest residence hall floor, the basement. The story goes that a young lady student committed suicide. One morning, her lifeless body was found hanging from a silk scarf. The reason for the student's suicide was never known, as it went to the grave with her.

There have been many bizarre occurrences in the basement of East Hall. Since that day, there have been reports of the sound of a girl's whispering voice. Balls of light near the ceiling in some rooms have been seen. A freshman named Perry was with his girlfriend one night when they saw a strange figure standing near his roommate's bed. A freshman named Bell was trying to get a nap when a picture flew across the room, shattering on the floor.

Some students have reported being pushed by an unseen hand. One student said that he felt a hand pushing against his forehead. Students have reported cold spots when moving around in the basement. A strange glowing blue mist about the size of a human was seen in the basement. It was moving through walls, always returning to the bathroom where the student hanged herself.

WAMPUS CAT

The legend of the Wampus Cat is still alive and being told throughout the mountains of Western North Carolina and East Tennessee. Strange things happen in the mountain valleys at night. Screams and howls and other strange noises echo through the darkness. There is something roaming the hills of Western North Carolina when darkness falls.

Animals disappear from farms. Things left in the yard are moved around or destroyed. Whenever strange things happen or a mysterious sound is heard coming from the woods, people are quick to put the blame on the Wampus Cat.

There are several different legends as to what the Wampus Cat really is and where it came from; of course, no one can agree on a date. One source says the first half of the nineteenth century. Another source says it first started appearing in the twentieth century. No matter who's right, there is something out there.

The most common legend comes from the Cherokee Indians. According to the laws of the tribe, it was forbidden for the Indian women to hear the scared stories or see the magic that was performed before the hunting trip. The Indian braves would always sit in the woods by the campfire and ask forgiveness for the lives of the animals that they were about to kill.

The curiosity of a beautiful Cherokee woman got the better of her. She wanted to know the scared rites. One night, when the Indian braves, along with her husband, set out on their hunting trip, she wrapped herself in the skin of a wild cat, mountain cat or cougar depending on the source. She

hid nearby and watched. As she slipped closer to the men, she was taking in every detail until the tribal sorcerer or tribal medicine man or shaman saw her. For breaking the scared rites, the sorcerer cast a spell on the woman. The cat skin she was wearing became her own skin, turning her into a half woman, half cat. She was doomed to roam the Appalachian Mountains forever, never to enjoy the company of humans again. If you are wandering the Appalachian Mountains at night and hear a strange cry resembling a cat, you've heard the Wampus Cat.

One source says she resembles a cougar but walks upright with red or yellow glowing eyes and fangs.

BLUE GHOST FIREFLY

The Blue Ghost Firefly (*Phausis reticulata*)—or lightning bug, depending on where you're from—makes its appearance from the last week in May through about the second or third week in June. They're thickest between 9:30 p.m. and 10:30 p.m. They prefer a moist environment and appear right above the ground, usually below knee level. They stay lit for several seconds to as long as a minute. Some say they resemble elves carrying blue candles. They don't flash—they glow.

They make their yearly appearance in Transylvania and Henderson Counties in Western North Carolina. This tiny little bug only shows up in a few places on Earth. The Blue Ghost Firefly is about the size of a piece of rice. It only appears during mating season. The female Blue Ghost glows, but since they don't have wings, they can't fly like the male.

The Blue Ghost Firefly was first discovered by botanist Thomas Nuttal and first described in scientific literature in 1825. It is said that they showed up in several southern states—Georgia, South Carolina, Tennessee and North Carolina. A paper published in 2010 noted that Blue Ghost Fireflies show up in the Appalachian Mountains in large numbers, especially in the DuPont State Forest. However, other forests have them too, including Pisgah, Tremont, Sherwood Forest and Connestee. However, their habitat is shrinking. Now they're relegated to a few Appalachian forests with spongy leaf bottoms.

The forest located between Hendersonville and Brevard is 10,400 acres of Blue Ghost habitat. The Blue Ghost is fragile and lives in the spongy leaf

litter on the forest floor. It spends most of its life in larval form. After mating and laying eggs as an adult, the firefly dies.

Fireflies become silent when cellphones, cameras, flashlights or a full moon or any other light source drown out their mating call. Development in Transylvania and Henderson Counties is destroying much of the Blue Ghost Firefly habitat.

Blue Ghosts have a legend connected to them that says they are the spirits of Confederate ghosts, but since they glow blue, wouldn't they be more likely the ghosts of Union soldiers?

In my younger days, we would sit on the porch, waiting for a flash and then rushing toward it trying to catch a lightning bug. If you were lucky, you might just catch one. You looked at it in your cupped hands and then let it go to repeat the process all over again. That's how we ended our summer days in the South.

Lightning bugs evoke a fairy tale magic that captivates audiences everywhere.

GHOST OF
CRAVEN STREET BRIDGE

The French Broad River slowly runs through Asheville, North Carolina, and ends up in Tennessee. In the early days, when rivers were important transportation routes, it was the French Broad River that connected North Carolina to the west. The French Broad River runs slowly through Asheville, making it the perfect place for a swim on a hot summer day. There is an unusual story that is connected to the French Broad. It is the story of the naked ghost of Craven Street Bridge.

In the early twentieth century, a group of young boys decided to go for a swim in the French Broad. The boys were in the western part of Asheville where Interstate 240 now crosses the river. It was the days before bathing suits were fashionable. Many people didn't own bathing suits, especially young boys. The boys stripped down to their birthday suits and dove into the river. As the boys started swimming, they failed to realize that strong currents due to recent rains were pushing them farther away from where they had entered the river. As the sun was sinking low and darkness was quickly approaching, the boys realized that they were in trouble. They had drifted into dangerous water, where Craven Street Bridge crossed the river. They knew they needed to head home, but one boy was missing. They frantically searched for the missing boy, but in vain. They sent one of the boys to the neighbors for help. Someone summoned the authorities. Everybody joined in the search. Those who had boats put them in the river. Lanterns lit up the river. Others searched the banks with lanterns. The search continued into the next day. It was a long, exhausting search, but the boy's body was never found.

Shortly after the boy's disappearance, strange things began to happen near the bridge. People traveling across the bridge just before dark reported seeing a naked boy running alongside of their car and then vanishing before he crossed the bridge. Some have called out to him, but he pays them no attention—it's like he doesn't hear them. He just keeps running and disappears.

Naked ghosts are very rare in the history of American folklore. Why ghosts have clothes on has been a hotly debated subject in religion and the paranormal. If the spirits of the dead are the souls returning to earth, then why are they wearing clothes? Do clothes have some immortal element that lets them return with the spirit? How do we know that if and when a soul returns to earth it will be in human form? How do we know that the spirit or soul returns to earth at all? How do we know that it won't be a light or a shadow? These and many other questions need to be answered before the question of "Do ghosts really exist" can be tackled.

AVERY COUNTY BIGFOOT

It was November 15, 1975, 1:00 a.m., and two friends were cruising on the Blue Ridge Parkway in Avery County, North Carolina. They had driven about nine miles toward Virginia when they noticed something large in the middle of the road. They drove to within ten to fifteen feet of the animal. It stood up on two feet in the middle of the road.

One of the friends was an avid hunter and immediately realized that this was no bear. The creature stood upright seven to eight feet tall and must have weighed between four and five hundred pounds. It had broad shoulders with long arms reaching almost to its knees and was covered in black fur. It was kind of hunched over at the waist. It walked away into the woods and out of sight. They couldn't see its face because it kept it turned away from the car lights.

At about the same time of this sighting, people were having problems in North Cove with something scaring their dogs. They detected strange odors and noises.

AVERY COUNTY BIGFOOT, 2010

On November 9, 2010, at about 3:30 p.m., there was a daylight sighting of Bigfoot near Linville River Bridge in Avery County, North Carolina. The weather was sunny, and the view of the river was good.

The witness lives in Forest City, North Carolina, and works near Linville at a resort. He stated that he was very familiar with the bears in the area. He was driving home from work between forty and fifty miles per hour and had to cross Linville River Bridge. He saw an animal standing upright on two feet in the middle of Linville River. This was about a mile from the Linville Wilderness and Falls area. It was about one hundred feet from the bridge. It was a large, dark, chestnut-colored animal.

The witness hit the brakes to slow down and startled the animal. It was standing sideways facing in the direction of his travel. The animal turned its head and looked in the direction of the man. From his estimates, it was more than seven feet tall and had short hair. There was not much hair on the face. Its arms were longer than a normal man's, and they seemed to reach to the animal's knees. It appeared to be very muscular. The sighting lasted about five to eight seconds. The witness drove on but then turned around and went back, but the animal was gone.

MYSTERIOUS ACTIVITY IN THE GREAT SMOKY MOUNTAINS NATIONAL PARK

On July 12, a two-foot-deep fissure, likely caused by the weather, was discovered cutting a Blue Ridge Parkway road in two. There was nothing unusual about that—just another natural occurrence.

However, there was another road closure that was not caused by the weather northeast of Asheville. This road was in the Great Smoky Mountains National Park. Some say that strange things were going on there.

Sixty miles west, near Cherokee, repeated road closures brought with them strange happenings. Beyond the barricades, residents began reporting loud booming and grinding sounds. Mysterious residues and heavy vehicle and air traffic were only the start. No construction had been seen despite the booming sound above and below ground.

Residents who traveled into the park on foot or ATVs were stopped and turned back by armed men. One person who walked through the woods to take pictures began feeling sick.

Some residents reported finding odd residue on their property following airplane fly-overs. Some of the residents developed respiratory problems. Some reported hearing heavy equipment movements in the park, including tractor trailers hauling odd structures.

The activities were centered near Balsam Mountain, North Carolina.

HENRY RIVER GHOST TOWN

In 1904, Michael Erastus Rudisill laid out a mill and village on 1,500 acres. That tract of land was chosen for the potential of its hydropower.

Rudisill—along with his brothers Albert Pinkney Rudisill and Miles R. Rudisill; David Williams Aderholdt; and Marcus Aderholdt—built the village, the dam and the mill building. In 1905, a thirty-foot concrete dam was built along with a three-story brick mill building.

In 1905, a textile mill was built outside Hildebran, North Carolina, along the Henry River in eastern Burke County. The mill produced fine cotton yarn and was powered by water via a giant waterwheel until 1914. For the following twelve years, it was powered by steam. Then, in 1926, it was completely switched over to run off electricity.

The Henry River Mill Village was an active community. It had a company store, a boardinghouse, thirty-five individual homes, a schoolhouse, a church and a moonshine still. Henry River had its own currency. Half of the millworkers' pay was in currency that could be spent at the company store. Henry River produced its own electricity and had a fire protection system in place.

In 1973, the mill closed its doors. The last resident left town in 1987—the town of Henry River was officially a ghost town. In 1976, the mill was bought by a private owner who was hoping to reopen it. In 1977, the mill caught fire and burned to the ground. The late Wade Shepherd owned the Henry River mill village property.

In 2012, Hollywood thought that the run-down village would serve as the perfect setting for the post-apocalyptic dystopia of District 12 in *The Hunger Games*. The Henry River village was featured in several scenes. Wade Shepherd put the entire town up for sale for $1.4 million.

The ghost town of Henry River has always been rumored to be haunted from the time it was abandoned in 1987. Often when people approach the first building, something is thrown at them from inside the building, usually a small rock or stick. People who have walked down the path leading down to the dam hear voices of multiple men talking. Another story is that if you stand there long enough, the men will turn toward you and stare at you with a grin.

Since 2003, the Henry River Mill Village Committee has been looking into working with the owner to devise a way of preserving the mill village. The owner had closed off the place due to vandalism. Do not go on the property without permission from the landowner.

WITCH BALL

A witch ball is a hollow sphere of plain, colored or stained glass. In eighteenth-century England, witch balls were hung in windows to ward off evil spirits or protect against witches' spells.

The witch ball originated among cultures where witches were considered good. Witches were once revered as healers. The witches would enchant the witch ball to enhance their power to capture or ward off spirits. The magic behind the function of the witch ball varies depending on where you are located. All legends agree that it's the color or beauty of the ball that attracts the evil spirits. The colors mesmerize the spirits. When the spirit touches the ball, the ball absorbs the spirit and traps it within the webbed strands of glass inside. Witch balls are traditionally green or blue, but in recent years, other colors have become popular. Other legends states that evil witches are lured to the ball because of their sparkling colors. When the witches enter the ball to investigate, they become trapped for all eternity.

Another legend notes that the witch ball attracts negative energy in the air. The ball should be displayed in the house, maybe in the bedroom or kitchen, to help rid the house of evil spirits. After a negative energy or evil spirit becomes trapped inside the ball, it may be exorcised by wiping the dust off the ball. Witch balls are believed to have been around for more than six hundred years. The witch ball was first used during medieval times to ward off witches, goblins and evil spirits. During Victorian times, witch balls were displayed to show prestige and wealth.

Witch balls have many different names and legends surrounding their existence, depending on the location and time in history. Some are known as fairy orbs. Instead of attracting negative energy, they attract fairies and good luck, as the orbs remind the fairies of flowers.

Spirit balls are similar to witch balls except they have an open hole. In colonial times, people believed that the spirit ball would protect the home from evil spirits. The colorful surface would attract the evil spirit, which would fly inside the ball and become trapped in the glass strings.

Good luck balls are given as wedding or housewarming gifts to bring the recipient luck, happiness and good health.

Gazing balls have a reflective surface and are usually one solid color. According to legend, the gazing ball attracts evil spirits and witches, but because they can see their reflection on the ball, they are scared away instead of being captured.

It is sometimes claimed that the modern Christmas ornament ball is a direct descendant of the original witch ball. The legend goes on to say that the ornament was hung from the tree to dispel a visitor's envy of the presents under the Christmas tree. However, the modern Christmas ornament is documented in Lauscha, Germany, in 1847. Thus the legend of the Christmas ornament being a descendant of the witch ball is debatable.

As you travel around the Carolinas, you can see these gazing or witch balls in many homes, flower gardens or just sitting out in yards.

BIGFOOT DNA

Real or hoax? Many times over the years, Bigfoot hunters have said that they had proof that there are Bigfoot creatures, but each time their evidence has been debunked by scientists. Since the first sighting of Bigfoot or whatever that mysterious and elusive creature might be, there has not been one conclusive bit of evidence to back that up. Is Bigfoot, like many other things, being covered up by the government?

Genetic testing allegedly confirms that the legendary Bigfoot is a human relative that arose some fifteen thousand years ago. A company called DNA Diagnostics issued a press release detailing the supposed work of a Texas veterinarian. The report from S. Ketchum suggests that such cryptids mated with human females and the end result was a big hairy hominin hybrid. Where's the evidence? There is none. The scientific community is dubious about Ketchum's claim.

Ketchum's research has not appeared in any peer-reviewed scientific journal. No outside experts have been able to examine Ketchum's evidence. For Ketchum's study, three whole nuclear genomes from purported Bigfoots were obtained, but Ketchum refused to let anyone see her evidence.

The history of Bigfoot is filled with exaggerated, premature and outright false claims about proof. The evidence has always been a hoax, a misidentification or inconclusive. No one outside Ketchum's team knows how, from where or by whom the alleged Bigfoot DNA was collected. It could have been collected by top forensics experts or by amateur Bigfoot hunters with no evidence gathering training.

How did they collect the sample DNA? Did they get it from a Bigfoot? If so, where are the pictures? If they found a sample, how do they know it came from a Bigfoot? It could have been left by another animal or a human, as far as that goes. The sample could have been compromised. Let's not forget another little item: there's no Bigfoot DNA to compare it to therefore there cannot be a conclusive match.

YANCY COUNTY BIGFOOT

August 21–22, 2011, two brothers and their friend were camping in the Black Mountain Campground in Pisgah National Forest near Busick, North Carolina. They were camping just to the east of the Smoky Mountains National Park near the Blue Ridge Parkway.

On the first night, they heard strange yells out in the woods just after dark. Later that night, the three of them were sitting around the campfire playing dominos when they heard another yell. This time, they could tell it was much closer, and they heard something rustling in the woods nearby. They couldn't distinguish what it was because some people were singing hymns at a small theater nearby.

Later that night, when everything was quiet, one of the boys was asleep, while the two brothers were talking about the upcoming nuptials of one of the brothers. The younger brother said that he saw something moving through the woods near the campsite. The following morning, he told the others about his sighting during the night. Back in 1994, one of the boys, while in the Boy Scouts in New Mexico, had seen a Bigfoot and was a little worried that it may be a Bigfoot there.

That day, the two brothers went on a long hike while the other boy stayed at camp. While sitting there with nothing to do, he got bored. He decided to go for a walk down a game trail—or at least what seemed to be a game trail. He got several hundred yards away from camp and started noticing that a lot of small trees were broken. He continued to walk until he was maybe a fourth of a mile from camp…and then he saw it. He couldn't determine how long he watched the thing—maybe fifteen seconds to a minute. He described it as very heavy with long, dark hair. The witness said that he was between fifteen and thirty feet away from it. They stared at each other for the duration of the sighting, and then it just turned and walked away like it had nothing to worry about.

After describing it to the two brothers back at the camp, the one who had seen something the night before said that it was just like what he had seen.

HAUNTED
NORTON CREEK TRAIL

The Norton Creek Trail is located in the Great Smoky Mountains of North Carolina. The Norton Creek Trail starts at the north shore of Fontana Lake at Lake View Drive. It goes six miles upstream to the upper and lower Norton Cemeteries. The trail is an old roadbed that's still in use today, but only during Decoration Days, when the families of those buried in the cemeteries meet to celebrate their ancestry and decorate the graves.

Many places in the Great Smoky Mountains are rumored to be haunted, but the Norton Trail is said to be the worst. The trail has the most concentrated number of ruins and cemeteries in the whole Great Smoky Mountain Range.

The Great Smoky Mountains National Park probably has more ghost stories per square mile than any other national park in the United States. Along the trail, you'll pass a number of historic sites with ruins, among them chimneys, stone walls and crumbling foundations. There are supposedly more than two hundred known cemeteries remaining inside the national park. The largest concentration of these cemeteries is on the north shore of Lake Fontana. There are several places you can camp along the trail, if you have the nerve.

The Legend of Spearfinger

Undoubtedly the scariest story along the Norton Creek Trail is that of an old Cherokee legend, Spearfinger. This story begins way before the settlers invaded America. Spearfinger has been called a witch and even an ogre.

The Cherokees called her U'tlun'ta, which translates as "Spearfinger."

Perhaps the Cherokees told this story to keep the children from wandering off into the woods. Perhaps there's a more sinister reason behind the legend. The legend goes that Spearfinger is a witch that lived on the highest ridge in the Smoky Mountains. She had one long finger made of stone and as sharp as a knife. It seems that if children wandered off, Spearfinger would lure them

to her house. She'd rock them to sleep and then use her finger to cut out their livers. She would steal the livers of her victims painlessly and without them knowing it. The children would continue on their way, only to later die a mysterious death.

Supposedly Spearfinger was a shapeshifter. She would troll the trails of the mountains disguised as an elderly grandmother in order to lure children who wandered too far from their village. She could change her appearance to anyone she wanted, but she preferred to look like a kindly grandmother.

The villagers finally decided to get rid of Spearfinger. They dug a pit and filled it with sharp sticks pointed up and then covered it with weeds and grass so she couldn't see it. She returned to the village disguised as an old grandmother, but she didn't fool the villagers. They started shooting arrows at her, but they had no effect. They ran, and she gave chase, only to be led to the pit. Not seeing it, she fell in. The spikes had no effect on her either. She was trapped, but nothing they did had any effect on Spearfinger. Two birds flew down and tried to help. The first was a titmouse singing "um," which meant heart. The villagers started shooting at her heart, but this had no effect on the old witch. The second bird, a chickadee, landed on her hand. The villagers shot her hand. With the help of the little birds, that was the end of Spearfinger, as her heart was in her hand.

THE LIGHT

A settler went into the woods searching for his daughter who had disappeared. The settler was killed. This happened near one of the small communities that once existed on the north shore of Lake Fontana. Over the years, hikers who have wandered off the trails and gotten lost have told stories of seeing a ghostly light that led them safely out of the woods. The light is believed to be the spirit of the man who was killed searching for his daughter. Is he doing a good deed from the grave? WGHP Fox8 rated the Top Ten Haunted Hiking Trails in America. Norton Creek Trail was number one.

LOST COVE

There's something magical about a ghost town in the middle of the woods—decayed buildings, stone chimneys standing all alone and other remnants of a bygone era serve as a reminder of more vibrant days of a long-forgotten time. Lost Cove ghost town located in Yancy County, North Carolina, is just that.

The last family said goodbye and moved away in 1957. Now the self-sustaining community lies in shambles, stricken by time, the elements and, of course, vandals. When the last family moved, they left small graveyards dotting the area. Some markers are still in place and legible.

Lost Cove was settled just after the Civil War and went on to become a great logging, agriculture and railroad community. When Prohibition came, Lost Cove found another calling as a haven for moonshiners who were making moonshine.

Lost Cove never had electricity or running water. The only way in or out of Lost Cove was by passenger train or a long walk down the railroad tracks. Once passenger trains stopped running in the 1950s, residents would have to walk eight miles to get to Poplar, North Carolina, to purchase needed goods or sell their goods or to see a doctor.

Situated in towering 5,000-foot-high mountains, Lost Cove lives up to its name, hidden away 2,500 feet up in the mountains. Now hikers have to follow the railroad tracks up to visit the ghost town. It's not an easy hike.

In December 2012, the Southern Appalachian Highlands Conservancy (SAHC) bought a ninety-five-acre portion of historic Lost Cove in the

Nolichucky Gorge. Lost Cove is one of the most legendary ghost towns in the eastern United States.

Another story that goes along with the legend of Lost Cove is that two families from a Daniel Boone expedition originally settled the area.

Today, only a few structures remain in Lost Cove. One structure is said to be haunted by one of the Lost Cove residents. People who go inside the house are said to get an uneasy feeling.

MOON EYED PEOPLE

The Cherokee Indians remember a race of white-skinned people who lived in the mountains long before the white man arrived. Cherokee legend says that this group of beings was known as the "moon eyed people." They were small and had pale white skin, blond hair, large blue eyes and were, some sources say, bearded. The legend says they were called moon eyed people because their eyes were so sensitive that they could not see in the daylight but could see very well at night. For this reason, the moon eyed people were underground dwellers. When the Cherokees and moon eyed people met, war broke out. The Cherokees won the war and expelled the moon eyed people from their land.

In the southern Appalachian Mountains from North Carolina through Georgia and Alabama are the remains of ancient stone structures that line the ridges. Some are natural rock formations, while others are entirely man made. Who built these structures and for what reason? Are these structures all that's left of the moon eyed people? According to several sources, they were built around AD 400–500.

Another legend finds the moon eyed people being driven from their home by the Creek tribe from the south. The Creek caught them during a full moon, when it was too bright for the nocturnal cave dwellers, and drove them into parts unknown.

The Cherokee legend of the moon eyed people has been matched to the time of the legend of Welsh prince Madoc. According to the Welsh version of the story of Madoc ab Owain Gwynedd, he was disenchanted with the war

that was going on in his homeland. Prince Madoc, his brother Rhirid and a select few of the Welshmen who followed Madoc sailed across the Atlantic Ocean in 1170. They landed somewhere around present-day Mobile Bay, Alabama. Madoc liked the New World and decided to leave Rhirid and a few of his fellow Welshmen behind. Madoc sailed back to his country and recruited more followers. They later returned to America. Neither Madoc nor any of his people were ever heard from again. Some speculate that while Madoc and the Welshmen were exploring the New World they ended up in North Carolina and that the moon eyed people were descendants of the Madoc colonists.

The moon eyed people were mentioned in a 1797 book by Benjamin Smith Barton. Barton also claimed that the moon eyed people created the area's pre-Columbian ruins that were left after their defeat. Barton's source is a conversation he had with Colonel Leonard Marbury (1749–1796).

Another author, Barbara Alice Mann, suggested that the moon eyed people were Adena Culture people from what is now Ohio who merged with the Cherokee Indians around 200 BC.

Reverend Morgan Jones claimed that he was captured by a group of people called Doeg in what is now present-day South Carolina in 1666 who spoke Welsh. He was later released.

According to a sixteenth-century manuscript published by Welsh antiquarian Humphry Llwyd, Prince Madoc sailed from Wales and landed in what is now modern-day Mobile Bay, Alabama, in 1171.

A soapstone carving of conjoined figures is on display at the Cherokee County Historical Museum. It is believed to be a centuries-old effigy that was apparently carved out, revealing two-headed, three-foot-tall conjoined figures with round eyes too large for their faces. The effigy was found in Murphy, North Carolina, in the early 1840s. It went on display for public viewing in 2015. The figures are believed to depict the moon eyed people. They look like nothing else ever found in the Southeast. Another theory is that the moon eyed people were alien beings from some far distant planet. Kind of far-fetched, or is it?

The fate of the moon eyed people remains one of the many unsolved ancient mysteries. The truth lies buried somewhere in antiquity.

WEAVERVILLE UFO

This sighting happened on July 26, 2017, at 10:00 p.m. and lasted between ten and fifteen minutes. A couple were sitting on their second-story deck looking northeast toward the mountains. There were no visible houses or lights in the area where they were looking. On this moonless night, with a starry sky, three large, sparkling red lights became visible. They were in the valley in front of the mountains. The lights were in a vertical row and were stationary.

After a minute or so, they noticed two more red lights rise up from behind the trees and position themselves side by side with the other three lights. Another red light appeared at the bottom just above the trees, making six red lights. The top light disappeared. Then, in sequence of their appearance, they disappeared. A lone red light appeared over to their left briefly before disappearing. The lights did not reappear.

RUTHERFORD COUNTY BIGFOOT

This sighting was on March 15, 1991, in Rutherford County, North Carolina. It was midmorning and drizzling rain. The reporting witness and his brother-in-law were trout fishing in the Broad River area of Bat Cave, North Carolina. The reporting witness was standing on a large rock in the middle of Broad River. He had been at that location for about thirty minutes when something on the other side of the river caught his attention. He saw something standing on two feet looking at him. There was a distance of about forty feet between the witness and the thing. They looked at each other for about ten seconds, and then it turned and walked up the mountainside. After about twenty steps, it was hidden from view in the bushes. The witness's brother-in-law was about fifty feet downriver and saw the same thing.

It was between six and eight feet tall, weighed about three hundred pounds and was covered with dark, brownish gray hair. Its hair appeared to be several inches long. Its cheeks, eyes and the palms of its hands were bare but were about the same color of its hair. Its arms were longer than a person's would be at that height.

The reporting witness owns a roofing company in Asheville, North Carolina, and is very familiar with the animals in the North Carolina mountains.

MACON COUNTY BIGFOOT

This Bigfoot sighting was experienced on June 15, 1985, in Macon County, North Carolina. A boy was walking up an old logging road heading to the top of the mountain on the border of Nantahala National Forest. The boy walked around a curve and saw a creature squatting as if it was getting something out of the creek that crossed the logging road. The boy froze as it stood up. It looked directly at him and then turned and went down the logging road. The witness was about twelve years old. He and his family were on a camping trip at their cabin located near Cullasaja Gorge. The boy panicked and ran back down the logging road. The boy was about forty yards from the creature when he saw it. The best the boy could describe the creature was that it was about seven feet tall, with brown hair and long arms; it walked on two feet.

LIGHT ON THE
BLUE RIDGE PARKWAY

Bill, his wife, her sister and her husband decided to take a trip to Asheville. They lived in Cherokee, North Carolina, and had a free weekend. It's a fairly long drive, so they did some shopping, had something to eat and saw a movie. They left the theater after the movie was over at about 11:00 p.m.

It was a nice summer night, so they decided to take the Blue Ridge Parkway from Asheville to Soco Gap on the way home to Cherokee. Taking this route would double the traveling time.

The Blue Ridge Parkway was almost deserted, the sky was clear and the moon was shining bright. As they passed the Black Balsam overlook, the driver noticed a light on the road behind them. After a minute or so, they noticed it was glowing red. As they drove on, the light got closer and closer to them. The driver motioned for the rest to look back.

They all saw the red light. The light had gotten closer now, about two hundred yards back. The light was much higher off the ground than car or motorcycle lights would be. The light was illuminating the trees on the side of the road. It seemed to be just below the treetops. The light stayed with them and seemed to be chasing them down the parkway.

Ahead, they could make out the silhouette of the Devil's Courthouse, which meant they were coming up on a tunnel. Would the light follow them through the tunnel? The light was still about two hundred yards behind them.

They entered the Devil's Courthouse tunnel, and seconds later, the light entered the tunnel. Everything was bathed in red light. As they exited the tunnel, they pulled into the Devil's Courthouse parking lot. The light just flew past them, staying on the parkway, and then went up just over the treetops and headed down the northern side of the mountain. Everything was dark again.

THOMAS DIVIDE LIGHTS

Ghosts, spirits, swamp gas, ball lightning and car headlights—the hypotheses continue to grow. What is behind this strange phenomenon along the Blue Ridge Parkway? Some other explanations include combustible methane gas or fireballs thrown by the legendary Cherokee giant Judaculla. Another legend speaks of the lights of lanterns carried by the Cherokees' mythical Little People. Of course, let's not leave out UFOs.

It starts with a drive down the Blue Ridge Parkway to the Thomas Divide overlook at mile marker 464. When you get there, you just sit and wait. If you're lucky, you will see the lights. The lights of yellow and white move across the ridge, sometime stationary while other times they move rapidly across the ridge. Sometimes they stay for a long time. Sometimes they never appear. Sometimes you can see the lights on your first visit, while others never see them. The story of the Thomas Divide lights has been told for generations.

The Cherokee elders, many of whom have passed on, claim that they heard family stories of the lights as far back as the 1700s. The elders believe that the lights are the guardians of the mountains.

Another story is that the lights flicker on, shine brightly for a few minutes and then flicker off. When the lights reappear, one light might divide into two, and another light will change colors from white to blue to blood red.

Another legend goes that when the government ordered the removal of the Cherokees from the mountains, many escaped into the mountains but were tracked down by the soldiers. When the soldiers caught up with the witch doctor or shaman, they executed him as an example to the others. The shaman's body was dismembered and spread throughout the mountains. Another legend has it that the soldiers would capture the witch doctor or the shaman's family and would kill them if the witch doctor or shaman didn't turn himself in. When he did, the soldiers would kill his family anyway. The legend is that the lights are the spirit of the witch doctor or shaman trying to find all of their parts.

The Thomas Divide lights are North Carolina's least-known ghost lights. There is very little documentation on the lights. The lights appear brighter in the winter.

Of course, there's always some silly ritual that you have to do to get the lights to appear, such as flashing your bright lights or honking your horn. There's the ritual where you yell at the lights to make them appear. Neither these nor any other ritual has ever been known to work. Are the spirits just sitting around waiting for us humans to do something stupid? Boy can we ever.

PEGGY BUCK

I couldn't find much information on the Peggy Buck Legend. It's a good story, so I decided to include it in this book.

From high up on a remote section of western Wilkes County comes the haunting legend from the 1780s. It's not a ghost story. It's a tragic tale of a mother and her starving baby. Eighty-seven-year-old Imogene, who grew up in the Big Ivy area, had this to say: "Peggy Buck ain't no ghost story and she ain't no witch."

According to the legend, Peggy Buck was a young unwed mother. After finding herself with child, she fled into the shadows of Big Ivy to get away from her mean father. Soon after the baby was born, Peggy realized that she was unable to nurse her baby. Realizing that her baby was going to die, she made a deal with the devil. Peggy was standing at the edge of the north prong of Lewis Fork Creek. She begged the devil to give her milk to feed her dying baby. The north prong of Lewis Fork creek is close to where an old steel bridge now stands at the intersection of Walsh and Big Ivy Road.

When the deal was made, the baby grew a full set of teeth just like a demon. The baby was so hungry that it starting biting chunks out of Peggy's face and hands. The baby kept eating right down to the bone. Now Peggy Buck was so disfigured and scarred that she was able to scare any man or animal to death.

Imogene said, "She learned herself by watching how to turn into all kinds of animals and demons so she could hunt better food." Some say Peggy slept under the crook of a rock by the creek. Others say she stayed down by the

water hole because she was trying to wash her sins away. One day, Peggy was down at the hole washing the demon baby when a big buck deer stopped by for a drink. Peggy was starving, having been without food for weeks, and dropped her baby in the water to grab the buck by the horns and drown him. While drowning the buck, the baby also drowned.

Here comes another ritual. A father and son went down to the area to try to summon Peggy Buck. They called out her name, and a deer ran in front of the car. Again they called out her name, and they had to stop before hitting a ground hog. A third time they called out her name, and a rabbit ran in front of the car. They decided it was time to go home. If you go down to Peggy's Hole and whisper her name three times, she'll come screaming for you too.

Whether Peggy's a shapeshifter, a witch, a devil woman or a murderer, her legend lives on in Wilkes County. This story, or a version of it, has been handed down for more than two hundred years. Each time the story is told, the macabre details ebb and flow like the chilling waters of Peggy's Hole.

In the 1990s, John and Jane Maddocks bought the 180-acre farm and heavily wooded property. Peggy's Hole was cited on the deed. The hole is about twenty feet wide, twenty-five feet long and a little over six feet deep. "It's really a lovely spot," said John Maddocks.

This place is on private property.

BFRO INVESTIGATOR
WITNESSES BIGFOOT

This Bigfoot sighting is a bit unusual due to the fact that the person witnessing Bigfoot is a Bigfoot Research Organization field investigator in the mountains of Western North Carolina. The investigator has lived in the North Carolina mountains all his life.

On Tuesday, June 23, 2015, he decided to take a drive to his research area. He was on the main road about five miles from his destination. As he was going around a slight curve in the road, a coyote on the side of the road caught his eye. He slowed down, and to his left he saw the creature just off the road. It was standing behind the guard rail. As the truck lights hit the creature, the investigator got a good look at it. He went on until he could turn the truck around and go back to the area of the sighting. He stopped and searched the area. He could not find any signs of the creature.

The creature had reddish-brown hair with gray-white hair underneath. The hair was shaggy looking. The creature stood upright and was very tall. The shoulders were very large, and the head was slightly forward with no neck. The witness remained in the area for about four hours, but nothing else happened. There were no other witnesses. The weather conditions were good, and the moon was out somewhat.

The road he was traveling on runs through the Nantahala National Forest and has some major curves and hills on it. He was traveling thirty to thirty-five miles per hour. The time was 11:50 p.m.

GHOST OF CHICKEN ALLEY

One of the most haunted cities in North Carolina is Asheville. Things get pretty spooky at night in this historic mountain city. There's one place that if you go there after dark, you may get a good scare.

Chicken Alley is a small, narrow alley in downtown Asheville. It got its name because of the chickens that would gather in the alley in the earlier days. These days, you won't see any stray chickens in downtown Asheville. The only chicken you'll see in Chicken Alley is a large mural of a chicken painted by local artist Molly Musk. The big chicken casts a cool stare on passersby, coaxing them to stop for another look. Some even wander into Chicken Alley. That is exactly the purpose of the big chicken. It gets people to go back into the agricultural past.

In the 1900s, a family ran poultry processing plant on that block. As all evidence of the poultry processing plant disappeared, and so did the chickens.

The mural of the giant chicken adds a bit of color to the alley, which some people say has something much darker lurking in there. Many say it's a non-poultry presence. They say it's the ghost of Dr. Smith. Residents of this alley claim that it houses a ghost that has been around for more than one hundred years.

Dr. Smith was a prominent physician in Asheville around 1902. He was known for wearing a wide-brimmed black fedora hat and a long duster coat. He always carried his medicine bag and a cane.

With the logging industry nearby, the loggers would come to town on the weekends to spend money, drink and have a good time. Dr. Smith was by

no means a stranger to good times. The town provided whiskey that flowed like water and brothels to draw the men in and keep them happy. Dr. Smith spent most of his doctoring time treating ailments caused by the sins of the day—social disease and injuries from barroom brawls.

In 1902, Dr. Smith walked into Broadways Tavern, which was located in Chicken Alley. There was a barroom brawl going on at that time. Dr. Smith tried to break it up but was stabbed in the heart. He died instantly. Dr. Smith's murderer was never caught. A year after Dr. Smith's death, the Broadway Tavern burned down.

For more than one hundred years, people who live in Chicken Alley and those just passing through say they have seen a man wearing a wide-brimmed black fedora and a long duster coat lurking in the alley late at night. He is heard frequently tapping his cane as he walks. Dr. Smith's ghost is seen between Carolina Lane and Woodfin Street in the short alley.

MUSEUM OF
ASHE COUNTY HISTORY

The building that now houses the Museum of Ashe County history was constructed in 1904. It served as Ashe County's first courthouse until 2001, when Ashe County built a new one. The old courthouse faced an uncertain fate. It had been patched up for as long as anyone could remember—would the old relic be demolished or saved?

For a dedicated group of Ashe County citizens, demolition was not an option. The old courthouse had to be preserved. The group joined together to save the patched-up old building as a museum.

The Ashe County Historical Society, members of the Ashe County Board of Commissioners, the county manager and the New River Community Partners worked together to get a grant from the North Carolina Department of Transportation. If the grant came through, the county agreed to match the funds. Together they created the Museum of Ashe County History Inc. to restore the building.

The museum listed the Virginia Creeper railroad as a priority exhibit to satisfy the Department of Transportation requirements for a relationship to transportation. The Virginia Creeper was once Ashe County's link to the outside world.

The Museum of Ashe Country History Inc. is a nonprofit organization. Its purpose is to turn the Ashe County courthouse building into a museum. The structure is the museum's number one exhibit. When the courthouse was built, it had Beaux Arts style with Classical columns and a cupola roof. The façade resembles a Greek temple and a sacred edifice. The foundation is made with native stone. The windowsills are made out of soapstone mined in Ashe County. The bricks were handmade in Mr. Baker's Brickyard. The framing timber was cut on the north slope of Mount Jefferson.

Ashe County, North Carolina, lies in the northern corner of the state, where it meets the eastern tip of Tennessee and southern Virginia. The county seat is Jefferson, named for Thomas Jefferson in 1799. This site has long been suspected of being haunted. It was reported in 2010 that a summer intern, working alone on the first floor, heard the phone ring on the second floor. Then the intern heard footsteps walking across the floor in the direction of the sound.

On Friday evening, June 5, 2011, as dusk fell on the museum, the paranormal group 3P Paranormal began to unpack its high-tech ghost hunting equipment and prepare for a long night. The members were granted permission to do a ghost hunt by the museum's governing body. The team set up four stationary infrared cameras and used electromagnetic field detectors (EMF). Infrared thermometers were also included among their innovative cache of ghost hunting equipment.

The museum's curator, Don Long, joined the team. Long had heard countless stories about employees who reportedly had seen some paranormal activity. Long said, "There has always been ghost stories of folks who work there in the old days."

The team divided into two groups and took turns canvassing the building. The paranormal team captured an audio recording of a voice saying "order." It also recorded sounds of a gavel banging in the courtroom. In the same room, the sound of heavy footsteps and breathing were also recorded. Voices were also picked up in some other rooms. There appears to be some residual energy in the old courthouse.

BLUFF MOUNTAIN DEVIL

Bluff Mountain is located in Madison County, North Carolina. It lies along the state line between North Carolina and Tennessee. It is a prominent landmark for Madison County, North Carolina, and Cocke County, Tennessee. The Appalachian Trail goes across the top of Bluff Mountain and works its way down into Hot Springs.

There are no roads to the top of Bluff Mountain, so the mountain remains remote and provides a rich plant and wildlife habitat. The mountain features striking rock outcrops, pristine streams and waterfalls. The area is rich in trail access. A walk around Bluff Mountain offers scenic beauty, unusual land forms and an extraordinary botanical variety.

Bluff Mountain is part of a local mountain chain characterized by a substrate of mineral-rich rock called hornblende gneiss. Bluff Mountain is home to more than four hundred different species of plants, including the Indian Paintbrush, Gray's Lily and the world's only known population of Bluff Mountain Reindeer Lichen. Bluff Mountain boasts twenty-five endangered, rare or threatened flowering plant species.

Every place has a mystery or legend attached to it—here, it is the legend of the Bluff Mountain Devil. Over the years, this legend has changed in minor details. One version lists the farmer as John Crebs, while another keeps the farmer anonymous. I'm going to refer to the farmer as John Crebs. In the story, he was either looking for a lost calf or getting ready to go to work.

While working his way through the rough terrain at Bluff Mountain, Crebs ran into a heavy, seemingly unnatural fog. He began smelling the odor of sulfur and heard a noise coming from a thicket ahead of him. He started feeling that something was wrong and began to move very cautiously. The devil made his way through the thicket and emerged from the fog, never taking his eyes of Crebs. The devil warned Crebs to never speak of this incident or he would die within three days.

Without looking back, Crebs ran home as quickly as he could. Once he was safe inside his house, he discovered that his hair had turned white. To explain his white hair, he told his wife about the encounter with the devil in the woods. Two days later, Crebs was found dead in his rocking chair. His death was never explained.

ULAGU, THE GIANT
YELLOW JACKET

The Nantahala National Forest located in Cherokee and Jackson Counties, North Carolina, covers more than 500,000 acres. In the forest, there is a gorge that was cut by the Nantahala River over millions of years. The gorge is so deep that the sun can only shine on the bottom in the middle of the day, when it is directly overhead.

The Nantahala Gorge has a Cherokee legend associated with it. It tells us that in the bottom of the gorge, hidden deep in a cave, lived Ulagu, a giant yellow jacket. This is a Cherokee story from the beginning of the history of the Cherokee Nation. There was a Cherokee village called Kanugalai. The Indian village had one big problem: Ulagu.

Ulagu terrorized the village of Kanugalai. In the Cherokee language, Ulagu means "The Boss." It could move through the air faster than any other insect or flying animal, creating a wind with its huge wings. Ulagu preyed on the people of the village. It would appear out of nowhere, snatch unsuspecting children from the village and carry them away. Ulagu moved so fast that the Cherokees could not hit it with their arrows or track it back to its home.

One day, a Cherokee had an idea. They would kill a deer, tie a rope to it and leave it out where Ulagu could find it. Ulagu took the bait, but the deer was so heavy that it couldn't fly as fast. The Indians were thus able to track it by the rope it was dragging. All the hunters in the village gathered together to follow it. They followed the rope for many miles before the hunting party came to the end of the Nantahala Gorge. There they say the

Ulagu flew down into a cave. When the hunting party got to the cave, they saw thousands of tiny Ulagu flying around outside the cave.

The hunting party gathered up brushed and blocked the entrance to the cave so the giant Ulagu couldn't get out. They set the brush on fire, and the smoke filled the cave, smothering nearly all of the Ulagu to death. Some of the ones flying outside of the cave got away and flew into the woods. That's how we got those pesky little yellow jackets today.

This story came from James Mooney's 1900 book *Myths of the Cherokee*. Mooney was an anthropologist who worked for the Smithsonian Institute's Bureau of American Ethnography. Mooney spent many years with the Cherokees, writing many books on the Cherokee Nation.

LODGE ON LAKE LURE

N estled in the beautiful Hickory Nut Gorge on Lake Lure is a lodge that was built in 1937 as a memorial to George Penn, a highway patrolman who was shot and killed in the line of duty. The lodge on Lake Lure was a retreat for state troopers and their families for many years. In 1990, it became a public inn. There are seventeen guest rooms. Breakfast and a sunset cruise is included with the price of the room.

There is a ghost story tied to the lodge on Lake Lure. Some believe that the spirit of George Penn has taken up residence in the lodge. His gentle spirit has been seen in room 4. No one knows why the spirit chose that particular room. Sometimes he just strolls into the occupied room. The guest thinks that it might be someone who went into the wrong room by mistake. He just walks around and then disappears through the closed door, leaving the usually shocked guest in the room alone.

A former innkeeper referred to the spirit as kind of naughty. He often steals the toilet paper out of room 2—and only room 2. Puzzled guests keep showing up at the front desk asking about their missing toilet paper. The spirit also moves flower arrangements around.

On one occasion, a guest said that he wished the spirit would do something. Just then, a glass goblet was thrown against the wall.

COWEE TUNNEL

On December 30, 1882, a cold Saturday morning in Dillsboro, North Carolina, thirty convicts working on the chain gang were assembled on the eastern bank of the Tuckasegee River. They were waiting on transportation across the river to the Cowee Tunnel. The convicts had been working on the tunnel for several months.

As the railroads pushed farther and farther into the mountains of North Carolina, the railroad company found it harder and harder to get workers. The railroad turned to the state for the solution. The state needed to get some convicts out of prison, so it leased convicts to the railroad. The convicts laid track and dug tunnels through the most inhospitable terrain in the eastern United States.

One of the groups of convicts was working on the seven-hundred-foot Cowee Railroad Tunnel. They were under the supervision of J.M. McMurray and E.B. Stamps. The convicts worked with pickaxes and shovels throughout the winter of 1882 to tunnel through the rocky mountain.

Every morning, the convicts would be shackled together at the ankle and loaded onto a boat for their journey across the Tuckasegee River. Thirty convicts got into the boat, like every day before. As the men grew weary of the boat, some convicts, scared that it wasn't going to make it, began to panic and pushed toward the front of the boat. With the constant back-and-forth movement, the boat rolled to one side and the convicts fell into the freezing river. Shackled together, the convicts desperately tried to keep their heads above the water and swim to shore. Their shackles pulled them to their deaths at the bottom of the freezing Tuckasegee River. Eleven convicts and guards who remained on the boat were swept downriver. Onlookers watched but made no genuine effort to help rescue the drowning convicts except convict Anderson Drake. He saved one prison guard, Fleet Foster. Drake would have been given a pardon except that night they found Foster's missing wallet and gun in Drake's personal belongings. Drake was sent back to working in the tunnel. Sam Pickett was credited with saving several men from drowning and was given a full pardon by Governor Jarvis. The twelve convicts and one guard who were swept downriver survived.

The lifeless bodies of the nineteen convicts who drowned were dredged from the bottom of the river on New Year's Day 1883. All were buried in an unmarked mass grave near the mouth of the Cowee Tunnel. Recent investigations speculate that they may have been buried somewhere else. An investigation ruled that the deaths were accidental. The number of victims varied with the different sources.

The *Raleigh Observer* described the Dillsboro accident as "[t]he most awful that has happened in any of the public works of this state."

Once the Cowee Tunnel was complete, the WNC was open for business. Over the years, the Cowee Tunnel has remained a spot for disasters. There were train derailments and cave-ins in the pitch-black blind curve in the middle of the tunnel. Legend says that that the incidents could be attributed to a curse Drake may have placed on the tunnel.

Inside the dark tunnel, streams of moisture fall down the walls from the ceiling. Could these be the tears from the nineteen men who drowned and were buried near the tunnel's entrance?

Over the years, people have reported noises emanating from the tunnel—the sounds of pickaxes and shovels. Others report voices echoing from inside the tunnel, while others still reported moans, screams and unexplained splashing coming from inside the Cowee Tunnel.

LAKE RHODHISS DEMON

Duke Energy built the Rhodhiss Dam in 1925. Lake Rhodhiss was created with ninety miles of shoreline. This pristine lake covers about 3,060 acres and is located at the foothills of the Blue Ridge Mountains in Western North Carolina. It is a reliable source of water for nearby cities Granite Falls, Lenoir, Morganton and Valdese North Carolina.

Lake Rhodhiss is a popular place for swimming, boating, water skiing and fishing. There are four boat access areas and one bank fishing area on the lake. The lake is home to a variety of species of fish.

Lake Rhodhiss has crystal blue water because the lake has a sandy bottom. The natural beauty around Lake Rhodhiss is breathtaking. Duke Energy has preserved more than twenty miles of shoreline and the mountains serve as a background.

There is only one record of the Lake Rhodhiss Demon that I could find. I'm not sure how true is. Maybe it's just a campfire tale, but I'll let you be the judge.

This is about a boy (age unknown) who went fishing with some of his friends. It was getting late, and the sun was sinking low. As he turned, he saw something. It looked like some kind of shadow. It shook him up a little, but he didn't mention it to anyone. When he got home from fishing, he found the door to his home closed—yet he remembered leaving the door open. That night, he began having bad dreams and was mumbling to himself. He reported to his family feeling a cold chill that night.

The second day, he coughed up a long black hair. The family didn't think much about that. While he was taking a nap, he did a backflip and stood there with his back bent and his hands and feet on the floor. There was a bad smell in the house. The family was getting a little worried.

He then began speaking Hmong and saying strange things. The family knew that something was very wrong. They invited a shaman to get rid of whatever had taken over the boy. The boy was speaking in a totally different language and had a different personality.

The shaman said it was the demon of a woman with long black hair. He said that he would not allow this possession and commanded her to leave the boy. The demon left.

ROAD TO NOWHERE

The road to nowhere started in 1945 out of Bryson City, North Carolina. As the road would have gone through an Indian burial mound, Cherokee Indians and the residents of the reservation had the construction stopped. It goes deep within the Smoky Mountains and ends with a tunnel. The road consists of a six-mile scenic drive with gorgeous views of the Smokies, but there's a dark past. There's a sign at the beginning of the road that reads, "Welcome to the road to nowhere, a broken promise 1943." Construction stopped in 1971 after only six miles of a planned twenty-six-mile-long road were completed.

It started in the 1930s and 1940s, when Swain County sold a large amount of private land to the federal government for the creation of Fontana Lake and the Great Smoky Mountains National Park. Another source notes that the road was stopped due to an environmental issue: unstable rock. The rock was also acidic, and contamination may have upset the aquatic life in local streams.

Hundreds of people were forced to leave their small communities that had been home to them and their families for generations. The only way to return was to walk or by boat.

The government flooded the land building Fontana Dam. The hydroelectric power provided by Fontana Dam was vital in helping the government to build the atomic bomb in Oak Ridge, Tennessee. Fontana Dam is the highest dam east of the Rocky Mountains at 480 feet tall.

The area that was flooded by the dam blocked many people from getting to their family cemeteries. The government runs a ferry from the south side of Fontana Lake so the people can visit their loved ones at the isolated cemeteries.

In February 2010, the U.S. Department of the Interior promised to pay Swain County $52 million in lieu of building the road. As of this writing, only $12 million has been paid to Swain County.

On maps, the road to nowhere is simply called Lakeview Drive. Don't be fooled by the light at the end of the tunnel—the road stops just beyond the tunnel's exit.

Besides the uniqueness and sometimes eerie day trip, those who take the trip will be treated to one-of-a-kind views of Fontana Lake and the Great Smoky Mountains.

People have reported that the closer they get to the tunnel, the more uneasy they feel. Some have taken pictures inside the tunnel and gotten images of ghost orbs. There was one report of a person seeing a robed figure beckoning to him. No one else in his party saw the figure. Others have reported that when they try to take pictures in the tunnel, phones and cameras start malfunctioning. When people leave the tunnel, the electronic equipment returns to working perfectly. One girl got scared, clung to her friend and closed her eyes only to hear a man whispering, "Heather open your eyes." One person reported that they saw people in the woods dressed in buckskins. The person yelled hello, but no one else in the group saw the buckskin-clad people in the woods. Another person reported that they felt hands on their sides pushing them toward the tunnel. Others have reported getting recorded EVPs (electronic voice phenomena).

ALIEN TECHNOLOGY IN NORTH CAROLINA

It is said that a Mr. Bartoo built a magnetron in the mountains of North Carolina and was in communication with an alien race. The aliens told Bartoo to move from New Jersey, relocate in North Carolina and acquire some land on the eastern side of Stone Mountain, where the ley lines intersected. Bartoo said that it was revealed to him by the aliens that he was one of them who had been ordered to assume human form so that he could carry out their plans for Earth.

He contacted several North Carolina real estate agents, explaining exactly what he needed and where he needed it at, regarding the ley line intersection. One real estate agent contacted him back and said that he had the perfect property for him.

Bartoo's next problem was building his house. When he put the word out that he was looking for help, people came with building materials and helped him build his house. After his house was completed, his next problem was getting the materials to build the magnetron containment building. Again people brought him building materials and volunteered to help him build a pyramid-shaped containment structure at the exact location the aliens had told him. He needed more material to build the magnetron—copper pipes, circular magnets, quartz crystals and acrylic circular plates—and again the people came through.

When the magnetron was finally complete, Bartoo invited his wife, daughter and friends to watch the magnetron work. They were instructed to watch the clouds as they traveled from west to east on top of Stone

Mountain. The wind changed direction, and the clouds started moving toward the magnetron. When the clouds moved over the top of the pyramid, they were sucked down into the pyramid as if they were caught in a spiraling vortex. Stone Mountain is located in Wilkes and Alleghany Counties in North Carolina.

This story comes from a report that is about twenty to thirty years old. It noted that the builder Mr. Bartoo, at least, is dead.

BOOJUM

Eagle's Nest Mountain towers at the southern edge of the Balsam Mountain range. Eagle's Nest was once home to the ill-fated Eagle Nest Hotel. The hotel was built in 1900 by S.C. Satterthwait, an eccentric developer from Waynesville, North Carolina. The Eagle Nest Hotel was located in Heywood County, North Carolina. The grand opening of the Eagle Nest was an event to behold.

Soon after the opening, hotel guests began hearing the story about a strange creature that lived in the area. The wooly beast stood seven to eight feet tall, and his body was covered with thick, matted hair except for his long, lean, humanoid face. It was not quite a man, not quite an animal. The creature was called Boojum, and it seemed to be harmless enough. However, it did have two human habits. The creature would hoard rubies and emeralds that were found naturally in the North Carolina mountains in one of his caves. He also liked to look at pretty girls. It was not uncommon for a girl to go swimming in one of the many creeks. From time to time, he could be seen standing at a distance watching her. He could often be seen from a distance standing on a rocky mountain cliff near dark and could often be heard moaning deep in the woods.

One day, Boojum saw Annie strip down to her birthday suit to take a bath in a pond under a waterfall. Annie heard the rustling of the bushes, looked up and saw the creature. Annie didn't run from the creature—she fell in love with him. She left her home and family to go live in the mountains with Boojum. Every now and then, Boojum would leave Annie and go deep

into the woods. If he was gone too long, you could hear Annie cry out. She sounded like a cross between a cat and a hooting owl. One day, Boojum left and never returned. Annie started pining away for Boojum.

Guests at the Eagle Nest would often hear her tormented cries. They would gather on the porch to listen. Annie soon became known as Hootin' Annie. The guests started complaining to the owner about hearing digging and grunting noises coming from under the hotel. Then one day it suddenly stopped, never to be heard again.

Annie became convinced that the owner of the hotel had captured Boojum. Old-timers believe that Annie was responsible for burning down the Eagle Nest in 1922 to cover Boojum's escape. Annie vanished and was never heard from again.

The legend of Boojum is a mysterious piece of Haywood County folklore. Big hairy creatures still roam the North Carolina mountains, but now they are called Bigfoot. Could Boojum have been a Bigfoot?

GROVE PARK INN

Asheville's Grove Park Inn has a well-deserved reputation as one of North Carolina's premier hotels. This massive granite resort offers a panoramic view of Asheville and the Blue Ridge Mountains. The inn was built by Edwin Wiley Grove and his son-in-law, Fred Loring Seely. Grove came to Asheville on his doctor's advice and decided to stay. The inn opened in 1913 and has stunning spas, 510 rooms and suites and world-class restaurants.

Grove made his fortune selling a malarial preventative called Grove's Tasteless Chill Tonic throughout the South. It was advertised as effectively disguising the unpleasantly bitter taste of its active ingredient, quinine. It was enormously popular at the time, when malaria was a problematic disease.

The Grove Park Inn has remained open and in continuous operation since it first opened. Ten presidents, from Woodrow Wilson to Barack Obama, as well as many other notable people, have stayed at the Grove Park Inn, including Thomas Edison, Henry Ford, Harry Houdini, F. Scott Fitzgerald and George Gershwin.

The most famous guest who stayed there—and perhaps stays there to this day—is the Pink Lady. She is the inn's resident and much-loved ghost. It is believed that she is the spirit of a young lady who fell or was pushed from the balcony on the fifth floor near room 545 in the 1920s. She fell from the fifth floor to the floor of the atrium two floors below. One source says she was staying with a registered guest in room 545 and fell from that balcony. She is said to be a friendly spirit with a kind heart.

The Pink Lady is often seen and felt in room 545. Guests and staff report seeing her appear as a pink smoky form. Some have felt her as a cool breeze or a static charge on their skin. Some have reported on rare occasions that she might tug on guest's ears. Guests in room 545 have sometimes been locked out of their room. Some have had the bathroom door locked from the inside. One guest was alone, sitting on the edge of the bed using the telephone, when he felt the other side of the bed sink in, as if someone had sat or lain down on it. Children of some guests talked about the nice lady in a pink dress that came in for a visit.

Sometimes she is seen as a full apparition of a young lady in a pink ball gown. She has been seen by the bed of sick children at the inn. In a more famous case, a doctor and his family had been staying at Grove Park Inn. When he checked out, he left a note asking the staff to thank the lady in the pink gown for playing with his children and how much they liked playing with her.

Some guests reported that they were woken up by the Pink Lady tickling their feet. She also enjoys turning the lights, air conditioners and various other electrical devices on and off. She has also been credited with moving guests' belongings around in room 545. The lady in pink has also been seen in the nightclub and in the lobby near the fireplace.

According to legend, she's the one guest that has never checked out.

OLD WILKES JAIL

Built in 1859, the Old Wilkes Jail is now a historical landmark in Wilkesboro, North Carolina. It was used during the Civil War to hold prisoners. Shortly after the war, the jail held its most famous prisoner, Tom Dula. Another famous prisoner held there was escape artist Otto Wood. Wood successfully escaped from ten different jails. The Old Wilkes Jail was the first one to keep him secured.

The Old Wilkes Jail was in operation until 1915, when it was sold. It was then converted into apartments. Fifty-three years later, the jail/apartment complex was scheduled to be demolished. A nonprofit organization in Wilkesboro heard the news and stepped up to buy the property. It successfully turned it back into its original design and layout as a jail. It still retains some of the original materials. The windows are from the Civil War and still have the original bolts that kept prisoners from escaping. A lot of the wood was preserved, along with the original door. The doors still have the nails intact that kept the prisoners from cutting through the door.

The old jail was opened to the public in the 1970s. Today, the Old Wilkes Jail serves as part of the Wilkes Heritage Museum.

You may have heard the song about Tom Dula (pronounced "Dooley"), based on the 1866 murder of Laura Foster that took place in Wilkes County. Tom Dula was accused of murdering Laura Foster. The story goes that Tom was in love with Laura and her cousin, Anne Melton. Anne, who was married at the time, was in love with Tom. Laura told Tom that she was pregnant. Tom and Laura were to meet in the woods and leave together. There was no happy ending to this love story. A search party was sent out after Laura's horse returned home without her. The body of Laura Foster was found—her legs had been broken, and there appeared to be a stab wound in her breast. Her body was taken to the nearest town, and her funeral was held. She was buried on a hill that is now known as Laura Foster Hill. Tom Dula was arrested and tried for the murder. Tom was found guilty and sentenced to hang.

When asked if he had any last words to say, Tom said, "I never hurt a hair on the girl's head." Then the trap was dropped. Tom was hanged on May 1, 1868, in Statesville, North Carolina. He was buried in a cemetery in Happy Valley near Elksville, North Carolina. Many suspected that Anne Melton may have murdered her cousin Laura. Some say that she confessed to the crime on her deathbed.

The story of Tom Dula became immortalized in the folk song "The Legend of Tom Dooley," which was passed around North Carolina for nearly one hundred years before the Kingston Trio made it famous in 1958.

There have been reports of EVP recordings, rattling chains, voices, people grumbling and things mysteriously moved from their original location at the Old Wilkes Jail.

RIVERSIDE CEMETERY

Riverside Cemetery was born out of a need for a cemetery in the area. The founder's names read like a historic document of Asheville, North Carolina. There were seventeen men serving as the original stockholders in the Asheville Cemetery Company.

Riverside Cemetery was created in 1885, and it was planned as a garden-style cemetery. The cemetery had low rates for grave sites for much of its early life, with some sites being as low as five dollars.

In the 1940s, Riverside Cemetery fell into a state of disrepair when the Asheville Cemetery Company ran out of money, due in part to the Great Depression and the passing of many of its original stockholders. Many Asheville residents began to wonder what the future of Riverside Cemetery might be.

In 1947, Joseph Selby wrote a letter to the *Asheville Citizen-Times* about the condition of the cemetery. He urged the city to buy it. In 1952, the Asheville City Council accepted an offer to buy Riverside Cemetery for ten dollars. The city took charge and went to work upgrading the roadway, clearing brush and correcting the setting of more than five thousand graves that had sunk several feet below ground level.

There are almost fourteen thousand people interred there now. The cemetery has room for twenty-five thousand plots. Many of the remaining grave sites have already been bought. When the last grave site is sold and the last person has been interred, it will still be kept up as a cemetery and a place for people to visit their dearly departed.

Riverside Cemetery is hallowed ground in Asheville. Some of the notables interred in the cemetery are the famed American novelist Thomas Wolf, who was buried there in 1938. William Sydney Porter (better known as O. Henry), known for his short stories, was buried there in 1910. Other notables buried there include Lillian Exum Clement, the first local attorney's name to appear on the ballot for the statehouse in 1920. Kenneth Noland, the noted painter and founder of the Washington Color School, was buried in 2010. Then there's Governor Zebulon Vance. Vance rose to prominence as a member of the Confederate army during the Civil War. He went on to become a U.S. senator and two-time governor of North Carolina. He was buried there in 1894. Isaac Dickson, the first black man appointed to the Asheville City School Board, is buried there. There are also the remains of eighteen German POW soldiers from World War I at Riverside Cemetery.

Riverside Cemetery is a regional tourism draw, hosting about thirty thousand visitors per year.

As for the ghost stories, not much in the way of ghostly activity is reported at the cemetery. However, witnesses have reported hearing gunfire and seeing a phantom Confederate regiment marching in formation.

BALSAM MOUNTAIN INN

Balsam Mountain Inn is located in the community of Balsam, North Carolina. It's always entertaining to take a trip off the main roads and visit the little villages along the way. The Balsam Mountain Inn is perched on a 3,500-foot gap dividing the towering Plott Balsam and Richland Balsam Mountain ranges. Each place you visit has a story of its own, and the Balsam Mountain Inn is no exception. Balsam is off the Blue Ridge Parkway, just off US 23/74. It was once a stop for the railroad passengers, who would stay at the Balsam Mountain Inn (then called Balsam Mountain Springs Hotel). Balsam Gap was once home to the highest passenger rail station in the East.

The idea for the one-hundred-room hotel was started in 1905, and it opened its doors in 1908. The Balsam Mountain Springs Hotel was built with extra-wide corridors for the guests' comfort. Its one-hundred-foot porches were perfect for the spectacular views. The excellent food at the inn led the inn to become known as the "Grand Old Lady of Balsam."

The community of Balsam once boasted four general stores, a post office, several churches, an Episcopal school and a train depot. Today, just a handful of buildings remain, including the old railroad hotel recently resurrected as the Balsam Mountain Inn.

The inn was quickly falling into disrepair. Merrily Teasley, an East Tennessee innkeeper, spotted it by accident. Teasley bought the inn and began the restoration of it. The Balsam Mountain Inn is now in the National Register of Historic Places. It is one of the few buildings of its grandeur left in North Carolina. It was restored by Teasley to the exact guidelines set by the U.S. Department of the Interior. In 1991, the first two floors were opened for guests. In 1996, the third floor was opened.

As with most old buildings, the Balsam Mountain Inn comes with its resident ghost. The ghost here seems to be an exceptionally friendly ghost attached to room 205. The doorknob turns in the middle of the night without anyone's help. The windows rise by themselves.

Another ghost story involves a man and his wife, who were spending the night in room 205 when she was woken up by someone rubbing her back. Her husband was still asleep. The ghost's identity remains a mystery. No deaths have ever been reported there. Unexplained footsteps are often heard when no one is present. The infrared door alarm in the entrance to the dining room and the alarm in the kitchen keep going off without any reason. The eye on the gas stove would sometimes be found turned on but not lit—the smell of gas would immediately be evident. An image of a person has been seen crossing in front of the cooler door as if they were walking from the laundry room to the dry storage room. When the dry storage room is checked, no one is there.

THE GIANT LEECH

The town of Murphy, North Carolina, is seated in an ideal, picturesque location at the mouth of a foothills gorge near the convergence of the Hiwassee River and the Valley River. At the northern end of Murphy is the spot known among the Cherokees as the Leech Place. Here there is a thin ledge of rock running across the Valley River that is just passable as a bridge. Just below this natural bridge is a deep hole in the bottom of Valley River where the water disappears into darkness.

The Cherokees used the bridge often until one day some Cherokees were going along the trail that led to the bridge. They saw a great red object as large as a Cherokee house lying on a rock ledge in the river. They saw it slowly unroll. When it stretched out, it was long, flat and looked fleshy. It looked like a giant leech. It was bright red with white stripes running along its body. It lay there for a while and then rolled up again and stretched out once more. It crawled off the rock and disappeared into the deep hole in the river.

The Cherokee legend says that after this, the water began to boil and foam. Then suddenly a great column of white spray was thrown into the air like a waterspout. The water landed on the spot where the Cherokees were standing. But the Cherokees ran out of the way before the water hit them and swept them into the river. This was the giant leech's trap. The giant leech would wait in the depths of the river for unsuspecting people to walk along the bridge. The leech would then send up a waterspout and wash them into the river. Many Cherokees were killed this way. Their bodies

would later be found lying on the riverbank with their noses and ears eaten off. The Cherokees feared crossing the bridge after this happened, afraid of becoming the giant leech's next victim.

One young Cherokee brave laughed at the story and made it plain that he was not scared of anything. He painted his face, put on his buckskins and headed for the river. Other braves followed at a distance. He went down the trail and out on the bridge. Before he was halfway across, things took a turn for the worse. The water began to bubble and boil into white foam. Then, without warning, a great waterspout swept over the bridge, carrying him into the water, never to be seen again.

Before the Great Removal, two Cherokee women went to the bridge to fish. One had a baby and laid it down on the ledge while she prepared her fishing line. The water started bubbling and swept over the bridge. The mother grabbed her baby, and the two women ran just before the water hit.

People still see something alive and moving at the bottom of the river. Some say there's an underground waterway across to the Nottely River where the river bends toward Murphy. Sometimes the giant leech goes over there and makes the water bubble and foam.

This story was adapted from James Mooney's 1900 work *Myths of the Cherokee*.

1889 WHITEGATE INN

The 1889 WhiteGate Inn is a well-known place to stay in Asheville, North Carolina. It has an AAA Four Diamond bed-and-breakfast rating, which is a very prestigious award. It is located on East Chestnut Street near downtown Asheville. Its red brick exterior, well-manicured lawn and gardens draw you in. The water garden and waterfalls that surround the perimeter set the mood for a very romantic getaway. It overlooks downtown Asheville and the majestic Blue Ridge Mountains.

The owners of the inn, Ralph Coffey and Frank Salvo, bought the inn in 1999 and worked hard to preserve the beauty and integrity of this historical building. The WhiteGate Inn is furnished with period antiques and other fine furniture. Some suites come with two-person Jacuzzi tubs, fireplaces, flatscreen TVs and Wi-Fi—or you can book the secluded garden cottage. There are eleven rooms, all named after poets. The inn has a greenhouse filled with more than 350 orchids and tropical plants. The gardens are home to fourteen varieties of Japanese maples and more than hundred different varieties of perennials, hostas and roses.

Christmas is a special time of year at the WhiteGate Inn. It's a winter wonderland. The inn goes all out, with Christmas decorations filing the parlor, solarium and living rooms with joy and the Christmas spirit.

The beauty of the 1889 WhiteGate Inn is not the only element that attracts visitors. Rumor has it that it's home to one of Asheville's most well-known spirits: Marion Bridgette, commonly referred to as "Miss B." Marion was the nurse who bought the home in 1928. Another source says that Marion passed way in 1928. Her room was the Robert Frost room.

Footsteps can be heard on the empty staircase. There have been reports of lights going on and off by themselves. Slamming doors have been reported. Cold spots have been recorded, and hot spots have been found in the Robert Frost room, the parlor and the basement. Floating orbs have been photographed in several places. Concentrations of electromagnetic energy have been identified.

1927 LAKE LURE INN

In 1902, Dr. Lucius B. Morse and his two brothers bought Chimney Rock Mountain and eight thousand acres joining the mountain. The mild climate here offers the ultimate in resort atmosphere. The area the Morses bought is located in the thermal belt in Western North Carolina.

Dr. Lucius Morse, who demonstrated what can be accomplished with a vision and a dream, was born in 1871 and grew up in Missouri. He attended medical school and was a practicing physician at Cooke County Hospital in Chicago, Illinois. He later developed tuberculosis and was advised to seek a healthier climate. He chose Western North Carolina.

In 1925, the concept of developing a lake in the valley below Chimney Rock at the foot of the mountain was being considered by several businessmen. Dr. Lucius Morse, president of Chimney Rock Mountain Inc., dreamed about what possibilities a lake could offer.

Dr. Morse owned the land and decided to flood the valley to make a lake. No one knows why his wife, Elizabeth Parkenson Morse, named the lake "Lure." In 1925, the Rocky Broad River was first damned, and by 1927, Lake Lure had been established.

Work began on the Lake Lure Inn in 1925. After construction on the inn was completed in 1927, it opened the same year. It is said that Dr. Morse did not live to see the grand opening of the inn. Behind the inn, Chimney Rock juts into the air. Not far behind it, water tumbles down more than four hundred feet at Hickory Nut Falls.

During World War II, the army commissioned the inn. The men serving during the war would stay at the inn to relax and recover from the wounds they received in the war. Five thousand combat airmen stayed at the inn in the 1940s.

The façade of the inn is pale yellow stucco, with hunter green shutters and a red shingled roof. Walk into the inn, and it's like time changes. Recent renovations have resurrected the past—original oak and pine floors, period furniture, oil paintings and bronze statues along with nineteenth- and twentieth-century music boxes that stand more than six feet tall can be seen in the inn.

F. Scott Fitzgerald frequently passed through the doors between 1935 and 1936. Calvin Coolidge visited the inn in 1928 as he neared the end of his presidency. Future president Franklin Roosevelt also stayed there. Patrick Swayze and Jennifer Gray stayed there while filming *Dirty Dancing* in 1986.

The charming Lake Lure Inn and the spectacular scenery are not the only attractions. It is reported to be haunted. Shadows have been reported by employees while cleaning the spa area late at night. One worker reported that while she was carrying some linen in the spa, she heard her name called by what sounded like a man with a low, gravelly voice. The worker made a hasty retreat to the supervisor's office. A supervisor was in the bathroom feeling a little sick when she heard someone say, "Are you all right?"

Guests have reported that a woman comes into their rooms at night and either tucks them in or will stand by the bed smiling. Some guests have left the room in the middle of the night.

One housekeeper reported on a Sunday morning that a lady in old-fashioned clothes walked by her. The housekeeper asked if she needed anything. The lady said no and floated on down the hall. The housekeeper quit. Other housekeeper have reported that glasses would break, TVs would turn on and off by themselves and freshly made beds would have an imprint as if someone had sat on them.

Night auditors have reported seeing a male figure in the dining room standing by the fireplace. They said it looked a lot like Dr. Lucius Morse—there's a painting of him hanging in the lobby. A smoky fog has been seen coming down the grand staircase.

Paranormal investigators have recorded EVPs of a woman screaming; another woman told the investigator to get out and called him by his name. The scream was recorded on two different occasions in room 217. A ball of energy was photographed in another room. In November 2010, the events manager took a picture of an ice sculpture. When the picture was more closely examined, there appeared to be an outline of a figure in the background. Things have been reported missing from guest rooms.

One guest reported that their daughter tripped and fell to the floor as she walked around the bed. She laughed and said that the bed had reached out and grabbed her leg.

GRANNY WITCH

The Appalachian Mountain Granny Witch magic tradition is a very old one. It dates back to the first settlers of the Appalachian Mountains. The settlers came from Scotland and Ireland in the 1700s. They brought their old Irish and Scottish healing traditions with them. These magical healing practitioners brought with them a wealth of healing knowledge and healing power. Appalachian folk healing goes by many names, depending on where it's practiced and who's doing the practicing—root work, folk medicine and kitchen witchery, among others. Most simply call it the work of the Lord.

The Appalachian Granny Witch Magic tradition was passed on from parents to children for generations. These medicinal secrets were not taught outside the individual family structure. Because of the nature of the Appalachian community, the old customs, wisdoms and practices were not lost in modern times. These magical women—healers of wounds, tellers of fortunes and hex casters—never considered themselves anything but noble, proud and God-fearing people. These people of the mountains still rely on Mother Nature in ways that city folks can't even imagine.

Amazingly, the term *witch* never became taboo in the modern Appalachian culture. Nearly every mountain and holler community has its local witch, a title of honor. The witches were called to heal the sick, deliver a baby or tend to the dying. Since there were no medical doctors in the mountain communities, witches were the only healers in the area. Many were seen carrying their little bags full of roots, herbs, berries and other essential things

needed to heal the sick. Granny Witches were critical in the care of the people in their communities. These women could do everything from talking the fire out of a burn to blowing on a wart—with a believing breath and a skyward nod toward the Maker, the wart would go away.

The Granny Witch is an example of the unique way mysticism and protestant Christianity overlap in the Appalachian Mountains. Whether it's rooted in the Bible, Mother Nature or good old-fashioned common sense, there's something enchanting about it all.

ASHE COUNTY HOSPITAL

The old Ashe County Hospital is located in Jefferson, North Carolina, at 410 McConnell Street. The hospital was built in 1939 and served as one of Ashe County's first hospitals. A lot of people passed away there from 1939 until it closed. In 1969, it was turned into a county office building. It was later closed completely.

The dark rooms inside the old hospital are well known for paranormal activity. The old building has been investigated by a number of paranormal groups. Each group reported finding paranormal activity there. Many investigators reported hearing disembodied voices that sounded much like doctors and patients going on like the hospital was still in operation. Some investigators reported that they have heard voices responding to their presence or asking questions. Images of ghostly mists have been seen around, and orbs have been reported in the hallways. There were also unexplained shouts heard at times.

Other people have reported hearing the sound of an elevator and the elevator bell even though there's no power in the building. Some reported that when they went into some of the rooms, they would get a chill.

Members of a group decided to use it as a haunted house at Halloween for a fundraiser. They had to add portable lights in the building since there was no electricity. They reported that lights would go out at nine or ten o'clock by themselves.

In 2016, the Ashe County Board of Commissioners unanimously approved a motion to involve county staff in a project to transform the old Ashe County Hospital into low-income housing for seniors.

SMITH-McDOWELL HOUSE

The Smith-McDowell House is one of the finest antebellum houses in Western North Carolina and the oldest brick residence in Asheville and Buncombe County. Situated on a ridge between two hills surrounded by picturesque mountains, Buck House, now known as the Smith-McDowell House, was built around 1840.

The three-story brick house was designed and built as a five-bay mansion in the Adamesque and Federal styles. The double-tiered front porch provides a great view of the mountain range to the southeast. The interior of the house contains much of the original Greek Revival woodwork.

The house is situated on a portion of a land grant issued to Colonel Daniel Smith after the Revolutionary War. The house was built by Smith's son, James McConnell Smith. James was born on June 14, 1787. James Smith was the first child of European parents born west of the Blue Ridge Mountains in North Carolina. James died in 1856, and his son, John Patton Smith, inherited Buck House. When John died in 1857, his sister and her husband bought the house and 350 acres of land for $10,000. It was kept in the family until 1951, when the Catholic diocese bought the house for a boys' school dormitory. In 1974, the Western North Carolina Historical Association leased the house and restored it over a six-year period. In 1981, it was opened as a house museum. Today, the Smith-McDowell House functions as the headquarters of the Western North Carolina Historical Association and a historic house museum. It is included in the National Register of Historic Places.

The Smith-McDowell House is reported to be haunted by two young girls, Sarah and Carrie, who died in the building. There is another spirit attached to the house called the Dark One, which is believed to be the spirit of a slave owner. Witnesses have taken pictures of a dark, misty entity and have heard someone call their names. Some people say that they have felt a cold presence, while others reported being touched by some unseen force in the basement.

GREEN PARK INN

Green Park Inn was opened in 1891 by three businessmen from Lenoir, North Carolina, including Civil War veteran Major George Washington Findlay Harper, who owned a large amount of land known as Green Park. Green Park Inn is located in Blowing Rock, North Carolina.

The original hotel consisted of more than seventy-three thousand square feet, three levels, a restaurant and a bar. It also had the only post office in the area. Part of the post office is still in the hotel.

The Green Park Inn often hosted famous and memorable people, such as Annie Oakley, J.D. Rockefeller, Eleanor Roosevelt, Calvin Coolidge, Herbert Hoover and world-famous writer Margaret Mitchell, who wrote part of *Gone with the Wind* while staying at the Green Park Inn.

The physical location of the Green Park Inn straddles the Eastern Continental Divide at the gateway to the Blue Ridge National Parkway. The Green Park Inn was placed in the National Register of Historic Places in 1982. The hotel is the second-oldest operating hotel in North Carolina.

Eugene and Steven Irace of New York bought the Green Park Inn in 2010. The hotel has eighty-eight guest rooms. Most of the hotel has been refurbished. The Carolina Room is a three-hundred-person conference and event room. The Blue Ridge Room is a smaller room, holding from fifty to sixty people.

The Green Park Inn is a member of Historic Hotels of America, the official program of the National Trust for Historic Preservation for recognizing and celebrating the finest historic hotels across America.

The *Washington Post* named the Green Park Inn one of thirteen haunted hotels across America. The story goes that Laura Green, daughter of one of the hotel's founders, killed herself or died of a broken heart in room 318 after she was jilted by her husband to be. (This cannot be confirmed.) Guests continue to report ghostly activity in and around room 318. There is allegedly a ghostly log in the lobby for visitors to report their encounters. Some guest report the aroma of pipe tobacco in room 318. Guests have reported that they saw Laura Green wandering the third floor. She is also known to disrupt electronic devices. There have been reports of ghostly children playing in the hallways of the Green Park Inn.

HIGH HAMPTON INN GHOST

In the mid-1800s, the Hampton family found comfort in what would become Cashiers, North Carolina, away from the heat of their native South Carolina. Wade Hampton III (1818–1902) built his own personnel retreat, the Hampton Hunting Lodge, just before the Civil War.

After serving as a general in the Civil War, Hampton returned to his lodge. He was sitting on the front porch when he received word that he had been elected governor of South Carolina. Hampton served as South Carolina's governor from 1876 to 1879.

In 1890, the Hampton property, including the Hampton Hunting Lodge, passed on to his niece, Caroline, and her husband, Dr. William Halsted. Halsted renamed the property High Hampton. He bought surrounding property from 300 acres to 2,200 acres up until his death in 1922.

Louisa Emmeline Zachary married Hannibal Heaton in the late 1890s, and with the marriage he gained possession of her property. Dr. Halsted wanted Hannibal Heaton's property and would pay well for the land. However, Louisa didn't want to sell the property. Louisa told Hannibal that if he sold her property, she would commit suicide. Heaton sold the land, and his wife, Louisa, killed herself. When Hannibal returned from selling the land, he found his Louisa hanging in the barn. As Heaton and his neighbors lowered Louisa's body, they saw a white-faced barn owl fly above her lifeless body. Her body was laid to rest at the Upper Zachary Cemetery. Heaton, distraught over his wife's death, tried unsuccessfully to commit suicide himself. In 1922, High Hampton was bought by E.L. McKee. Heaton moved from Cashiers to Franklin, North Carolina.

E.L. McKee built a two-story inn on the grounds. High Hampton Inn has 116 rooms and 17 guest cottages. There are no phones, televisions or air conditioning in the rooms, but there is a rustic southern gentility about the place.

A fire that started in a clogged flue of a fireplace destroyed the old hunting lodge and the inn in 1932. McKee built a new three-story inn on the site of the former hunting lodge.

Some say that Louisa Heaton returns in the form of an owl screeching at night. High Hampton Inn was the key location for the ABC television remake of the 1980s hit movie *Dirty Dancing*.

ASHEVILLE UFO

This sighting occurred on July 17, 1973, at about 9:00 p.m. and lasted for about four minutes. The object was huge and shaped like a disk. It was stationary and hovered at about fifty feet above the ground. The object had what appeared to be windows in the bottom, with an orange glow coming from them.

Steve (last name withheld from report) went for a drive with his wife and seven-year-old daughter. They were on a back road when Steve saw something floating in the air. It was a very dark night, but he had a good view of the disk. He stopped the car under the object, got out and stood under the thing. There was no noise coming from the disk. The object appeared to be as big as a football field. He watched it for a few seconds, and then the object started to move. It moved slowly at first, but then it darted about two miles in a few seconds. It stopped above a small mountain for a few seconds and then flew off about five miles toward some other mountains. It paused for a few seconds and then flew out of sight.

ASHEBORO UFO

It was around 9:00 p.m. on August 18, 2012, when the reporting witness (names omitted from report) went outside the Randolph Hospital to have a cigarette. He walked across the street to the smoking area. The lady who was already there asked him who was shooting fireworks. When the witness looked up, he saw twenty-five to thirty glowing orange balls up in the sky. The balls were getting closer and coming from the same direction. All of a sudden, they stopped and floated there for a few seconds and then moved off in different directions very fast for a few seconds. In seconds, they were gone. They moved at different intervals and were completely silent.

ASHEBORO UFO, PART II

This incident happened on September 10, 2014, at 10:15 p.m. The reporting witness (name withheld from report) was driving home from work; when he got about two miles outside Asheboro, North Carolina, on Interstate 73 and Interstate 74, he noticed something unusual. To his left, two or three miles ahead, there were two power line towers next to each other that had white lights on them. As he got closer, he noticed that something the color of turquoise was illuminated between the two towers. He could make out something that was about half the size of a blimp. As he continued driving and watching, it moved a little. He could now see a circle of red lights around it. When he got about a quarter of a mile from it, he could tell it was the shape of a sphere.

There were several cars on the road trying to see the sphere. Two cars pulled over, but he kept driving, fearing that someone would rear end him. He kept driving, hoping to get another break in the trees. The speed limit is sixty-five, but no one was doing it. They were driving about forty miles per hour. He took his exit. When he looked back, the object had taken off and headed west. It climbed high in the sky in a few seconds.

In about three minutes, what appeared to be an air force jet went by high in the sky in the direction of the object. He then saw ten North Carolina state troopers heading in that direction driving about a hundred miles per hour.

GHOSTS OF
PURGATORY MOUNTAIN

Purgatory Mountain is a low, flat mountain at the northern edge of the Uwharrie Mountain Range in Randolph County, North Carolina. The Uwharrie Mountains, some of the oldest in the world, span North Carolina in the counties of Randolph, Montgomery, Stanly and Davidson. The range's foothills stretch into Cabarrus, Anson and Union Counties and terminate in the hills of Pearson County.

In the spring of 1864, the Civil War was raging all over the South. North Carolina had been one of the last states to secede from the Union in 1861. The Quakers who lived in North Carolina were plain, hardworking people who opposed slavery and wanted to get along with everyone. They opposed violence of any kind. An order went out from the capitol that every able-bodied man was to enlist in the Confederate army. The men of the Quaker settlement were ordered to join. However, many Quaker men chose to go to prison instead of fighting.

To enforce this law, the state hired men to go around, take by force any men resisting the draft and bring them to serve in the Confederate army. One of the men hired to capture the Quakers was an evil, just plain nasty man who had murdered men before the war. They called him the Hunter. He was paid for every man he brought in. The Hunter set out for the Quaker settlement on a hill near Asheboro, North Carolina.

One version says the Quakers were gathered in their meetinghouse on Sunday morning when the Hunter burst in and pointed a shotgun at the Quakers. The young men of the congregation were captured. The Hunter

took twenty-two boys—some younger than fourteen—tied them together and marched them out of town at gunpoint.

Another version of the story says the Hunter arrived in the early hours of the morning as the Quakers were beginning their chores. Each home the Hunter went to, he took the eldest boy. The boys were hogtied and shoved in a wagon.

The boys were marched to the Port of Wilmington, where they received little to no training and whatever equipment could be spared. The boys were assigned to a regiment and sent into battle. Each night, they would camp in barns if they were available. If no barns were available, they would camp under the trees. The boys got what little food was available for supper. The soldiers who were guarding the boys walked away and left a knife. One of the Quaker boys put the knife in his boot.

As the guards went to sleep or passed out from whiskey, the boy got the knife out of his boot and freed himself and the other boys. The Quaker boys escaped and took the guards' rifles with them. Finally, after a month, the boys reached the mountain that marked the Quaker settlement. They hid out in the woods and at night would visit their homes and get food for the next day.

One night, they found out that the Hunter was looking for them and was camped on the other side of the mountain near Rich Field Creek. The Hunter vowed that he would not only kill every one of the boys but would also kill every one of the Quakers.

The boys held a meeting, where lots were drawn, and the three with the shortest sticks were chosen. The twenty-two boys vowed never to reveal the three chosen ones. That vow was never broken. Before dawn on that faithful day, the three boys left for Rich Field Creek, carrying the rifles they had taken from the guards. Just as the sun was coming up over the mountain, three shots were fired. The Hunter fell dead. The twenty-two boys avoided the mountain for the rest of their lives.

People began calling the mountain Purgatory Mountain. Some say that the ghost of the Hunter is destined to walk the mountain forever. In the early morning, just as the sun is coming up on the mountain, you can still see the ghost of the Hunter recruiting soldiers for his ghostly army.

Another version of the story goes that the boys set a trap for the Hunter, catching him in a snare. Using the rope that they had been tied together with, they hanged the Hunter from a high tree.

The terrifying ghostly figure of the Hunter has been seen in the woods on Purgatory Mountain. There is an unearthly fire burning in his eyes. It was for the ghostly figure of the Hunter that the mountain was named Purgatory—a dead man in neither heaven nor hell.

In 1971, Purgatory Mountain become home to the North Carolina Zoological Park. Another ghost story from Purgatory Mountain is about as strange as they come. Ranger Mike Yates worked the graveyard shift many years ago in the interim zoo. Yates was looking out of the security office window at the fog moving in. Everything outside was almost swallowed up by the ghostly fog. Yates went out to make his rounds. As he got into the truck, started it up and put it in reverse, he was startled when he looked

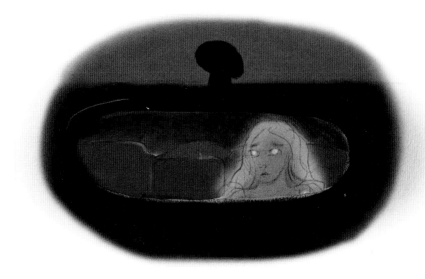

into the rearview mirror and saw an elderly woman in the glow of his brake lights. She was standing right behind his truck.

Yates jumped out of his truck to check on the lady and saw that she was dressed in formal clothes from years gone by. It was nearly 3:00 a.m. The elderly woman told Yates that she was here to meet someone. She then turned into the fog and started to walk away, heading toward the pond. Yates knew that in the dark and the fog, she could easily fall into the pond.

Yates called out to say that perhaps who she was meeting was waiting at the gate. He asked her to get in the truck so he could give her a ride to the gate. The elderly woman quietly got in. Yates drove her to the gate and saw an old car parked on the side of the road. The elderly woman got out of his truck, and Yates let her out the gate. The elderly woman walked over and got into the car. The car cranked up and started to drive away. Yates could not see who was driving it car. He decided to follow the vehicle and get the tag number. He lost sight of the old car for a few seconds when it went around a curve. When Yates went around the curve, the car had vanished.

Purgatory—an intermediate state after death for expiatory purification, specifically a place or state of punishment. According to Roman Catholic doctrine, the souls of those who die in God's grace may make satisfaction for past sins there and so become fit for heaven. Alternatively, purgatory is a place or state of temporary suffering or misery.

STRANGE APOCALYPTIC BOOMING SOUND

Whatever name you give them—Seneca Guns, skyquakes, sonic booms and now another name, apocalyptic booming sounds—they are heard all along the East Coast. Very little is written about the booming sounds being heard in the mountains of North Carolina. The Seneca Guns are perhaps one of the most mysterious legends the Appalachian Mountains have to offer. Scientists have no explanation for the sonic booms heard in the mountains. It seems that the legend is destined to join the mystery of Brown Mountain Lights as a phenomenon that occurs naturally with no other explanation.

The Seneca Indians passed down oral traditions that the lake guns were actually the angry shouts of their god Manitou. They passed on the stories of the booms in the 1600s and 1700s, long before the legend was created by the Europeans. The primary legend believed by the European settlers is that the booms are the ghostly remnants of the Seneca Indians still fighting for their land and their freedom.

In 1850, James Fenimore Cooper (1789–1851), an author from New York, wrote about Seneca Lake in the Finger Lakes of New York. He called the phenomenon the "Lake Guns" of New York.

The sonic booms are usually heard along the Carolina coastline, but they have been heard as far inland as Tennessee and Kentucky. Sometimes the sonic booms are so strong that they can be felt, along with the shaking the windows.

Scientists have come up with a few possible explanations. The booms are perhaps caused by enormous waves crashing against cliffs or sand dunes; meteors entering into Earth's atmosphere; or shock waves caused by coronal mass ejections from the sun crashing into Earth's magnetic field. Small earthquakes can transmit sounds of the planet's cracking crust. Of course, there's the old reliable one: methane explosions. There's also the theory that the booms are shock waves or sonic booms created by modern technology. There's only one problem with that theory: this kind of technology wasn't present in the 1600s.

David Hill, a U.S. Geological Survey scientist, noted that it's possible that some of the sounds originate from above.

Some seismologists have attempted to match seismic activity with reports of the booms. Their findings were that no earthquakes were happening during the times these booms were reported.

There are several other theories. There is the one about UFOs entering or leaving our atmosphere or the one about a UFO entering or leaving the ocean. Another suggests that Indian ghosts are firing guns to disturb the descendants of the settlers who took their land.

FAIRY CROSSES

Fairy crosses can be found throughout the Blue Ridge Mountains of North Carolina, Georgia, Tennessee and Virginia. Despite how frequently they appear in this region, fairy crosses remain uncommon throughout most of the rest of the world. Outside of the southern states, New Mexico is the only other state where they are found. These crosses are known by several names, including fairy stones and fairy tears.

Woodrow Wilson, Thomas Edison and Theodore Roosevelt are among those who believed that fairy crosses brought good luck.

In spite of all the legends and superstitions that surround fairy crosses, they do have a scientific explanation. Fairy crosses are formed in rocks that have been subjected to tremendous heat and pressure. These crosses are composed of staurolite, which is a combination of silica, iron and aluminum. Fairy crosses are formed naturally by a crystallization process. Staurolite crystallizes at sixty- or ninety-degree angles, giving the stones their cross-like structure. This mineral was formed long ago during the rise of the Appalachian Mountains.

These stones are most commonly shaped like a St. Andrews cross or the much less common T-shaped Roman crosses. You can still find fairy crosses sprinkled around in the Blue Ridge Mountains, often around bodies of water. The Cherokees believed that nature spirits inhabited the woods and that these little spirits crafted and left behind the stone crosses

Another Cherokee legend notes that the Cherokees shed tears of sorrow as they traveled the Trail of Tears. When their teardrops fell to the ground,

they formed tiny crosses of stone. Another Cherokee legend explains that fairy crosses are the fallen tears of the Yunwi Tsunsdi, or Little People— tiny fairy-like spirits known for their shy, timid nature and their ability to find lost people.

Many people believed that fairy crosses protected the bearer from witchcraft, sickness, accidents and other disasters. Another legend goes that the Little People were gathered together for a day of singing when a foreign messenger brought the news of the crucifixion. The story made the Little People cry, and their tears fell to the earth as small stone crosses. European settlers later adapted the magical legend to symbolize the power of Christ taking over the pagan magic of the indigenous tribes. The Europeans believed that the magical stones that appeared as crosses were a sign of Jesus's desire for the Europeans to preach Christianity to the Indians.

ONE LAST THOUGHT

I can't expect everybody to share my interests or want to engage in riddles from the past that interest me. I am intrigued by the mysterious, as I have been since I read my first issue of *Fate Magazine* forever ago. The world of the strange and unknown is fascinating, whether it's ancient cave markings, UFOs, aliens, ghosts or modern-day monsters such as the Loch Ness Monster in Scotland, Bigfoot, the Chupacabra or any other thing that defies a rational explanation. Are we any closer to understanding the riddles now than twenty years ago? No, we have not made any progress. There are a few of us who are dedicated to finding the answers. We can sit here and debate the fact that something exists or not forever and never come up with an answer. While we struggle with the realization that something exists, we just don't know what.

We are held prisoner by our way of thinking, relying on very little to no evidence to explain things. In our eternal pursuit of scientific evidence, we ignore other very important facts.

Ghosts, spirits or whatever handle you want to put on them have been around for as long as recorded history. We are no closer to finding out what they are than we were hundreds of years ago. Maybe we're using the wrong methods to investigate them. Legends are not built on nothing. They are not simply made up stories to entertain people. They always contain a modicum of truth. Our fascination with the unknown will keep those of us who have a serious interest in it looking for answers.

A lot of people would like to make you believe that they have proof that ghosts exists. This is the furthest thing from the truth. Photographic or video evidence can be manipulated, so that it would be inadmissible as proof. No proven scientific correlation exists between photographic anomalies and the paranormal, yet some still swear by it. There's no hard evidence that humans can communicate with the spirit world.

I invite you to open your mind and join me, immerse yourself in a world of the strange and unknown.

People grow up with their minds conditioned about ghosts. They have been taught that ghosts only come out at night and that Halloween is the most haunted day of the year. There's no proof that either of these is correct. In fact, most credible ghost sightings are during the daylight hours.

SOURCES

Sources by Story

DID THE DEVIL VISIT NORTH CAROLINA?: TOWN OF SEVEN DEVILS
blueridgencguide.com; sevendevils.net

DID THE DEVIL VISIT NORTH CAROLINA?: THE DEVIL'S COURTHOUSE
blueridgeheritage.com; cabinusa.com; romanticasheville.com;
stayandplayinthesmokies.com; Wikipedia

DID THE DEVIL VISIT NORTH CAROLINA?: THE DEVIL'S STAIRS
digital.lib.ecu.edu; facebook.com/carolinasunknown; geocaching.com;
hauntedstories.net; hauntin.gs

DID THE DEVIL VISIT NORTH CAROLINA?: THE DEVIL'S WHIP
mixsee.com; motorcycleroads.com

BROWN MOUNTAIN LIGHTS
brownmountainabductions.com; brownmountainlights.info;
brownmountainlights.org; Casstevens, *Ghosts of the North Carolina Piedmont*;
Coleman, *Dixie Spirits*; dancanton.physics.appstate.edu; Fitzhugh, *Ghostly
Cries from Dixie*; huffingtonpost.com; Little, "Brown Mountain North
Carolina Lights"; northcarolinaghosts.com; prairieghosts.com; pubs.usgs.

gov; Roberts, *Illustrated Guide to Ghosts*; Roberts, *Southern Ghosts*; Rogers, Mansfield Geological Survey Circular; romanticasheville.com; secretary. state.nc.us; Stephens, interview; Thay, *Ghost Stories of the Old South*; *USA Today*; westernncattractions.com; Wikipedia; Zepke, *Best Ghost Tales of North Carolina*

CAROLEEN BROAD RIVER BRIDGE
hauntedplaces.org; Newman, *Haunted Bridges*; northcarolinahauntedhouses. com; rumblingbald.com; strangeusa.com

HELEN'S BRIDGE
atlasobscura.com; asheville.com; rumblingbald.com; southernspiritguide. blogspot.com; Zepke, *Best Ghost Tales of North Carolina*

THE MYSTERIOUS JUDACULLA ROCK
atlasobscurra.com; geocaching.com; judacullarock.com; Mooney, *Myths of the Cherokee*; northcarolinaghosts.com; northcarolinahistory.org; stayandplayinthesmokies.com; Wikipedia

CHIMNEY ROCK APPARITIONS
Brown, *Haunted South*; northcarolinaghosts.com; onlyinourstate.com; remembercliffside.com; *The State Magazine* (August 1963)

GRANDFATHER MOUNTAIN'S PHANTOM HIKER
americanfolklore.net; northcarolinaghosts.com

SIREN OF THE FRENCH BROAD RIVER
ashevillelist.com; northcarolinaghosts.com; onlyinyourstate.com; sacred-texts.com

DILLSBORO VAMPIRE
beforeitsnews.com; hubpages.com; whatliesbeyond.boards.net

DEMON DOG
appalachianmonsters.blogspot.com; cdtechnology.wikispaces.com; mcdowellnews.com; northcarolinaghosts.com

HOT SPRINGS
ghostsofamerica.com; hotspringsnc.org; northcarolinaghosts.com; ourstate. com; prezi.com

SOURCES

DEAD DAN'S SHADOW
angelfire.com/in/lottgreene/hollostories.html; rumblingbald.com

THE PHANTOM RIDER OF THE CONFEDERACY
danswnh.storyblog.blogspot.com; hauntedstories.net; praireghosts.com

1907 ALTA PASS RAILROAD TUNNEL EXPLOSION
www3.gendisasters.com; *Bristol Virginia Dispatch*, May 13, 1907; *Washington Post*, May 14, 1907; *Statesville Record and Landmark*, May 17, 1907

1890 MELROSE TRAIN WRECK
Cranbury Press, June 27, 1890; www3.gendisasters.com

1948 ASHEVILLE HIGHLAND MENTAL HOSPITAL FIRE
Asheville Paranormal Society; Associated Press; *Florence Morning News*, March 12, 1948; National Register of Historic Places; nps.gov; *The Robesonian*, March 11, 1948; www3.gendisasters.com

1955 CHEROKEE FOOT BRIDGE COLLAPSE
bia.gov/cs; *Oakland Tribune*, July 4, 1955; United Press; www3.gendisasters.com

1916 LAKE TOXAWAY DAM FAILURE
aegcarolinas.org; laketoxway.com; *New York Times*, August 14, 1916

GHOSTS OF THE BILTMORE HOUSE
americashauntedroadtrip.com; biltmore.com; Brown, *Haunted South*; cbsnews.com; ghoststoriesandhauntedplaces.blogspot.com; hauntedstories.net; hauntedtravelsusa.com; hauntspot.com; nchistory.web.unc.edu; northcarolinaghosts.com

THE PHANTOM CHOIR
facebook.com; hauntedstories.net; northcarolinaghosts.com; rootssrated.com

THE BIGFOOT MYSTERY
bfro.net

APPALACHIAN STATE UNIVERSITY GHOST
The Appalachian, October 30, 2014; Brown, *Haunted South*; northcarolinaghosts.com

WAMPUS CAT
americanfolklore.net; appalachianhistory.net; mentalfloss.com;
northcarolinaghosts.com; Schlosser, *Spooky South*

BLUE GHOST FIREFLY
atlasobscura.com; blueridgenow.com; Cradle of Forest in America
Interpretive Association; DuPont State Forest; Kerns, *Hendersonville Times-News*; Lancaster, *Hendersonville Times-News*; ourstate.com

GHOST OF CRAVEN STREET BRIDGE
Llewellyn, *Haunted Bridges*; northcarolinaghosts.com;
northcarolinahauntedhouses.com; onlyinyourstate.com

AVERY COUNTY BIGFOOT
gcbro.com

AVERY COUNTY BIGFOOT, 2010
bfro.net; squatchable.com

MYSTERIOUS ACTIVITY IN THE GREAT SMOKY MOUNTAINS NATIONAL PARK
beforeitwasnews.com; skyshipsovercashiers.com; Whatley and Whatley,
Grey Area

HENRY RIVER GHOST TOWN
atlasobscura.com; carolinacountry.com; ghosttowns.com; Mickie Vacca,
executive director, Historic Burke Foundation; onlyinyourstate.com;
roadtrippers.com; *Voice of the Foothills*, February 2003

WITCH BALL
angeldelightspiritualreading.com; earthlorenews.wordpress.com;
homesandantiques.com; sunnyreflections.com; Wikipedia; witchball.co.uk

BIGFOOT DNA
Live Science; msnbc.msn.com; NBC News; *Technology and Science*

YANCY COUNTY BIGFOOT
bfro.net

SOURCES

HAUNTED NORTON CREEK TRAIL
blueridgeoutdoors.com; onlyinyourstate.com; theactivetimes.com; thegreatsmokies.net; werewoofs.com; WGHP Fox8, High Point, North Carolina; Williams, *Haunted Hills, Ghosts and Legends*

THE LIGHT
werewoofs.com; WGHP Fox8

LOST COVE
Fuller, *Johnson City Press*; onlyinyourstate.com; Southern Appalachian Highlands Conservancy

MOON EYED PEOPLE
allthatsinstering.com; ancient-code.com; ancientplaces.com; en.wikipedia. org; northcarolinaghosts.com; onlyinyourstate.com; roadsideamerica.com

WEAVERVILLE UFO
nuforc.org

RUTHERFORD COUNTY BIGFOOT
bfro.net

MACON COUNTY BIGFOOT
bfro.net

LIGHT ON THE BLUE RIDGE PARKWAY
ghostofbalsam.blogspot.com

THOMAS DIVIDE LIGHTS
Hester, *Western Carolinian*; Kasper, *Smoky Mountain News*; onlyinyourstate. com; southernspiritguide.org

PEGGY BUCK
Mitchelle, *Wilkes Journal Patriot*

BFRO INVESTIGATOR WITNESSES BIGFOOT
bfro.net

SOURCES

GHOST OF CHICKEN ALLEY
Brown, *Haunted South*; northcarolinaghosts.com; onlyinyourstate.
com; *Our State Magazine* (March 23, 2014); seeksghosts.blogspot.com;
strangecarolinas.com

MUSEUM OF ASHE COUNTY HISTORY
ashehistory.org; Campbell, *Ashe Post and Times*; Howell, *Ashe Mountain Times*;
northcarolinahauntedhouses.com; southernspiritguide.org

BLUFF MOUNTAIN DEVIL
Howell, *Ashe Mountain Times*; North Carolina Mountain Treasures,
Wilderness Society; The Nature Conservancy; wataugademocrat.com

ULAGU, THE GIANT YELLOW JACKET
Mooney, *Myths of the Cherokee*; northcarolinaghosts.com, Russell and
Barnett, *Mountain Ghost Stories*

LODGE ON LAKE LURE
hauntedplaces.org; southernspiritguide.org

COWEE TUNNEL
appalachianhistory.net; Baldwin, *Smoky Mountain Ghostlore*; ghostsofbalsam.
blogspot.com; onlyinyourstate.com; Woodward, *Smoky Mountain News*

LAKE RHODHISS DEMON
lakerhodhiss.org; yourghoststories.com

ROAD TO NOWHERE
atlasobscura.com; blueghostpost.blogspot.com; onlyinyourstate.com;
thebowenknot.blogspot.com; yourghoststories.com

ALIEN TECHNOLOGY IN NORTH CAROLINA
Filer's Files, #33, George A. Filer 111, 2018; globalwarming-arclein.
blogspot.com; nationalufocenter.com; nyufo.com

BOOJUM
ashevilleoralhistoryproject.com; folkmoot.org; northcarolinaghosts.com;
visitncsmokies.com

GROVE PARK INN
hauntedrooms.com; northcarolinaghosts.com; the-line-up.com; Zepke, *Best Ghost Tales of North Carolina*

OLD WILKES JAIL
blueridgeheritage.com; ncvisitorcenter.com; northcarolinaghosts.com; onlyinyourstate.com; theclio.com

RIVERSIDE CEMETERY
ashevilleparanormalsociety.com; Davis, *Asheville Citizen-Times*; hauntedplaces.org

BALSAM MOUNTAIN INN
ashevilleparanormalsociety.com; balsammountaininn.net; *Charlotte Observer*, October 3 2014; Ellison, *Smoky Mountain News*; ghostsofbalsam.blogspot.com

THE GIANT LEECH
firstpeople.us; Mooney, *Myths of the Cherokee*; northcarolinaghosts.com; technogypsie.com

1889 WHITEGATE INN
Asheville Press, October 16, 2016; bedandbreakfast.com; hauntedplaces.org; hauntedrooms.com; Melissa Locker, *Southern Living*; whitegate.net

1927 LAKE LURE INN
hauntedrooms.com; Jeremy Jones, *Our State Magazine* (October 1, 2017); McIntosh, *Mini History of Lake Lure*; meetup.com; onlyinyourstate.com; southernspiritguide.org; tripadvisor.com; yourghoststories.com

GRANNY WITCH
appalachianink.net; atlasobscura.com; witchvox.com

ASHE COUNTY HOSPITAL
allthatsinteresting.com; Campbell, *Ashe Post and Times*, September 30, 2010; hauntedplaces.org; highcountry.com; Howell, *Ashe Mountain Times*, July 5, 2016; Howell, *Ashe Mountain Times*, October 30, 2015

SOURCES

SMITH-MCDOWELL HOUSE
hauntedplaces.org; northcarolinahauntedhouses.com; nps.gov; wnchistory.org

GREEN PARK INN
americandreams.historichotels.org; greenparkinn.com; Meg Jernigan, *USA Today*; Miller, *Mountain Times*; hauntedrooms.com

HIGH HAMPTON INN GHOST
Asheville Paranormal Society; ashvegas.com; facebook.com; *Our State Magazine*; southernspiritguide.org; Williams, *Haunted Hills, Ghosts and Legends*

ASHEVILLE UFO
National UFO Reporting Center; robslink.com

ASHEBORO UFO
National UFO Reporting Center; robslink.com

ASHEBORO UFO, PART II
National UFO Reporting Center; robslink.com

GHOSTS OF PURGATORY MOUNTAIN
Asheboro Courier Tribune, October 30, 2018; northcarolinaghosts.com; *Richmond County Daily Journal*, October 10, 2012; Wikipedia

STRANGE APOCALYPTIC BOOMING SOUND
Baker, *San Diego Union Tribune*, May 19, 2015; candidslice.com; Carmichael, *Forgotten Tales of South Carolina*; Carmichael, *Legends and Lore of South Carolina*; Carmichael, *Mysterious Tales of Coastal North Carolina*; *Cosmos Magazine* (January 2, 2018); earthquake.usga.gov; lite987.com; snopes.com

FAIRY CROSSES
blueridgemountains.com; candidslice.com; sherpaguides.com; southernthing.com; spookygeology.com

ONE LAST THOUGHT
Von Daniken, *Impossible Truths*; Fitzhugh, *Ghostly Cries from Dixie*; Haze, *Ancient Aliens in the Bible*; *Hauntings in America*

Sources Overview

Books

Baldwin, Juanitta. *Smoky Mountain Ghostlore*. Virginia Beach, VA: Suntop Press, 2005.

Brown, Alan. *The Haunted South*. Charleston, SC: The History Press, 2014.

Carmichael, Sherman. *Forgotten Tales of South Carolina*. Charleston, SC: The History Press, 2011.

———. *Legends and Lore of South Carolina*. Charleston, SC: The History Press, 2012.

———. *Mysterious Tales of Coastal North Carolina*. Charleston, SC: The History Press, 2018.

Casstevens, Frances H. *Ghosts of the North Carolina Piedmont*. Charleston, SC: The History Press, 2012.

Coleman, Christopher K. *Dixie Spirits*. New York: Fall River Press, 2011.

Fitzhugh, Pat. *Ghostly Cries from Dixie*. Nashville, TN: Armand Press, 2009.

Haze, Xaviant. *Ancient Aliens in the Bible*. Wayne, NJ: New Page Books, 2018.

McIntosh, Carl. *The Mini History of Lake Lure*. Rutherfordton, NC: Liberty Press, 1993.

Mooney, James. *Myths of the Cherokee*. Mineola, NY: Dover Publications, 2012.

Newman, Rich. *Haunted Bridges*. Woodbury, MN: Llewellyn Worldwide Ltd., 2016.

Roberts, Nancy. *Illustrated Guide to Ghosts*. New Jersey: Castle Books, 1959.

———. *Southern Ghosts*. Orangeburg, SC: Sandlapper Publishing, 1979.

Russell, Randy, and Janet Barnett. *Mountain Ghost Stories and Other Curious Tales of Western North Carolina*. Durham, NC: John F. Blair, Publisher, 1988.

Schlosser, S.E. *Spooky South*. Guilford, CT: Globe Pequot, 2016.

Thay, Edrick. *Ghost Stories of the Old South*. Alberta, CAN: Ghost House Books, 2003.

Von Daniken, Erich. *Impossible Truths: Amazing Evidence of Extraterrestrial Contact*. London: Watkins Media Limited, 2018.

Williams, Stephanie Burt. *Haunted Hills, Ghosts and Legends of Highlands and Cashiers, North Carolina*. Charleston, SC: The History Press, 2008.

Zepke, Terrance. *Best Ghost Tales of North Carolina*. Guilford, CT: Pineapple Press, 2006.

SOURCES

Videos

Hauntings in America. Timeless Media Group, 2013.

Television

CBS.
MSNBC.
NBC.
WGHP Fox8.

Magazines

Comos.
Live Science.
Our State Magazine.
Southern Living.
The State Magazine.
Technology and Science.

Newspapers and Newspaper Articles

The Appalachian. October 30, 2014.
Asheboro Courier Tribune. October 30, 2018.
Asheville Press. October 16, 2016.
Associated Press.
Baker, Debbi. *San Diego Union Tribune,* May 19, 2015.
Bristol Virginia Dispatch. May 13, 1907.
Campbell, Jesse. *Ashe Post and Times.* September 30, 2010.
Charlotte Observer. October 3, 2014.
Cranbury Press. June 27, 1890.
Dillon, Davis. *Asheville Citizen-Times,* September 23, 2017.
Ellison, George. *Smoky Mountain News,* October 8, 2014.
Florence Morning News. March 12, 1948.
Fuller, Jessica. *Johnson City Press,* May 1, 2016.
Hester, Margaret. *Western Carolinian,* November 10, 2006.

Howell, James. *Ashe Mountain Times*, October 30, 2015; July 5, 2016.
Huffington Post.
Kasper, Andrew. *Smoky Mountain News*, January 23, 2013.
Kerns, Charli. *Hendersonville Times-News*.
Lancaster, Lindsay. *Hendersonville Times-News*.
Miller, Brian. *Mountain Times*, November 2, 2017.
Mitchelle, Laura. *Wilkes Journal Patriot*, October 31, 2017.
New York Times. August 14, 1916.
Oakland Tribune. July 4, 1955.
Richmond County Daily Journal. October 10, 2012.
The Robesonian. March 11, 1948.
Statesville Record and Landmark, May 17, 1907.
United Press.
USA Today.
Voice of the Foothills. February 2003.
Washington Post. May 14, 1907.
Whatley, Frank, and Kathy Whatley. *Grey Area*, July 19–August 1, 2013.
Woodward, Garret K. *Smoky Mountain News*. June 19, 2017.

UFO Organizations

Filer's Files.
National UFO Center.
National UFO Reporting Center.

Paranormal Societies

Asheville Paranormal Society.
Bigfoot Research Organization.
Carolina's Unknown.

Miscellaneous Sources

Cradle of Forest in America Interpretive Association.
DuPont State Forest.
Historic Burke Foundation.

Little, Dr. Greg. "Brown Mountain North Carolina Lights." Videotaped field observation, July 2003.

National Register of Historic Places.

The Nature Conservancy.

North Carolina Mountain Treasure, the Wilderness Society.

Rogers, George. Mansfield Geological Survey Circular, origin of the Brown Mountain Lights, North Carolina.

Southern Appalachian Highlands Conservancy.

Interviews

Stephens, Johnny. The Brown Mountain Lights. Interview by author.

Dictionary

Merriam-Webster

Web Resources

A

aegcarolinas.org

allthatsinstering.com

americandreams.historichotels.org

americanfolklore.net

americashauntedroadtrip.com

ancient-code.com

ancientpages.com

ancientplaces.com

angeldelightspiritualreading.com

angelfire.com

appalachianhistory.net

appalachianink.net

appalachianmonsters.blogspot.com

ashehistory.org

asheville.com

ashevillelist.com

ashevilleoralhistoryproject.com

ashvegas.com

atlasobscura.com

B

balsammountaininn.net

bedandbreakfast.com

beforeitwasnews.com

bia.gov

biltmore.com

blueghostpost.blogspot.com

blueridgeheritage.com

blueridgemountains.com

blueridgencguide.com

blueridgenow.com

blueridgeoutdoors.com

brownmountainabductions.com

brownmountainlights.info
brownmountainlights.org

C
cabinusa.com
candidslice.com
carolinacountry.com
cdtechnology.wikispaces.com

D
dancanton.physics.appstate.edu
danswnh.storyblog.blogspot.com
digital.lib.ecu.edu

E
earthlorenews.wordpress.com
earthquake.usga.gov
en.wikipedia.org

F
facebook.com
firstpeople.us
folkmoot.org

G
gcbro.com
geocaching.com
ghostsofamerica.com
ghostsofbalsam.blogspot.com
ghoststoriesandhauntedplaces.
   blogspot.com
ghosttowns.com
globalwarming-arclein.blogspot.com
greenparkinn.com

H
hauntedplaces.org
hauntedrooms.com
hauntedspot.com

hauntedstories.net
hauntedtravelsusa.com
hauntin.gs
hauntspot.com
highcountry.com
homesandantiques.com
hotspringsnc.org
hubpages.com

J
judacullarock.com

L
lakerhodhiss.org
laketoxaway.com
lite987.com

M
mcdowellnews.com
meetup.com
mentalfloss.com
mixsee.com
motorcycleroads.com

N
nchistory.web.unc.edu
ncvisitorscenter.com
northcarolinaghosts.com
northcarolinahauntedhouses.com
northcarolinahistory.org
nps.gov
nyufo.com

O
onlyinyourstate.com
ourstate.com

P
prairieghosts.com

prezi.com
pubs.usgs.gov

R
remembercliffside.com
roadsideamerica.com
roadtrippers.com
robslink.com
romanticasheville.com
rootssrated.com
rumblingbald.com

S
sacred-texts.com
secretary.state.nc.us
seeksghosts.blogspot.com
sevendevils.net
sherpaguides.com
skyshipsovercashiers.com
snopes.com
southernspiritguide.blogspot.com
southernspiritguide.org
southernthing.com
spookygeology.com
squatchable.com
stayandplayinthesmokies.com
strangecarolinas.com
strangeusa.com
sunnyreflections.com

T
technogypsie.com
theactivetimes.com
thebowenknot.com
thebrokenknot.blogspot.com
theclio.com
thegreatsmokies.net
the-line-up.com
tripadvisor.com

V
visitncsmokies.com

W
wataugademocrat.com
werewoofs.com
westernncattractions.com
whatliesbeyond.boards.net
whitegate.net
witchball.co.uk
witchvox.com
wnchistory.org
www3.gendisastors.com

Y
yourghoststories.com

ABOUT THE AUTHOR

Sherman Carmichael, a native of Hemingway, South Carolina, currently lives in Johnsonville, South Carolina. Carmichael has been dabbling into things that are best left alone since he was seventeen, like ghosts, UFOs, monsters and other strange and unusual things. He has seen, heard and felt things that defy explanation. Carmichael's first three books—*Forgotten Tales of South Carolina*, *Legends and Lore of South Carolina* and *Eerie South Carolina*—centered on ghosts and the strange and unusual. In his fourth book, *UFOs Over South Carolina*, Carmichael took a closer look at hovering objects and strange lights in the sky. His fifth book, *Strange South Carolina*, returned to ghostly encounters. Carmichael took a look at coastal North Carolina with *Mysterious Tales of Coastal North Carolina*. In Carmichael's seventh book, *Mysterious South Carolina*, he returned to South Carolina for more of the strange and unusual. In Carmichael's eighth book, he returned to North Carolina for more strange and unusual stories about the Piedmont in *Mysterious Tales of the North Carolina Piedmont*. Carmichael has traveled throughout the United States, visiting haunted locations, including Roswell, New Mexico. He has also traveled to Mexico and Central America researching the Mayan ruins. He plans to continue visiting these unusual places for many years to come. Carmichael worked for many years as a journalist, thirty years as a photographer, thirty years in law enforcement and twelve years in the movie entertainment business.

Visit us at
www.historypress.com